This edition published 1976 by
Mills and Boon Limited,
17–19 Foley Street, London W1A 1DR

ISBN 0 263 06012 8

Filmset by Ramsay Typesetters
(Crawley) Ltd, through Reynolds Clark
Associates Ltd, London
Printed in Italy by New Interlitho S.P.A.

Sure and Simple Series
created and produced by
Sackett Publishing Services Ltd,
104 Great Portland Street, London W1N 5PE

SURE & SIMPLE GARDENING

Geoffrey Smith

Illustrated by Sarah Kensington

Designed by
Keith Groom and Cyril Mason

Mills & Boon Limited

London

SURE & SIMPLE CONTENTS

SURE & SIMPLE GARDENING

Basic Gardening Tools

Before the owner of a new garden can do anything except contemplate the empty plot or make mental pictures of what the fruits of honest toil will look like, it is necessary to purchase a basic set of tools.

Gardening is a rewarding hobby but can be laborious and expensive unless the right equipment is purchased to take the ache out of the heavier work.

A *spade*, if possible made of stainless steel, is a prime requirement and with care should last a lifetime. A *fork* which, in addition to being used for digging, can double as a cultivator for breaking up hard clods of earth, lifting potatoes, dividing plants or spiking the lawn. A *rake* for reducing rough digging to a seed bed, clearing up debris, achieving levels when

sowing a lawn. A *push hoe* for weed control and aeration. A *trowel* for planting bulbs and seedlings. A *wheelbarrow* or large basket. A *wire rake* for lawn maintenance, removing dead grass and other unwanted material. A *garden line*, especially for keeping straight rows in the vegetable garden and edging up the lawn.

Hand shears are useful for hedge trimming and tidying up the herbaceous border; long handled shears for edging up after mowing. A *mower*, power or hand operated, cylinder or rotary, according to personal preference. *Secateurs* for rose and shrub pruning. A *hand cultivator* is another essential piece of equipment for keeping the soil loose and well aerated. Eventually a *shovel* for mixing compost, though a spade will suffice. A *shed* to keep all the garden equipment in — tools, fertilizer, etc; fish meal is not the sort of material any self-respecting housewife likes stored in the home.

Buy the best tools which the family budget will permit. Try each one personally in the shop before buying to see if it is right for balance and comfort. Never leave tools outside after use. Clean them and rub all metal parts with machinery oil; wooden handles may also be treated with linseed oil which brings up a beautiful sheen, making them comfortable to handle.

Secondary Purchases: A length of *hose pipe* and a *watering can* for periods of inevitable drought. A knapsack or hand *sprayer* to assist in pest and disease control. A *greenhouse* or small *frame*, which is the only medium which gives the gardener at least a minimal control over the climate for raising seedlings, pot plants, exotic fruits and vegetables.

7

Soils

Having bought the tools, only lack of inclination can prevent the home owner starting work on improving the garden.

Soils vary widely from area to area in texture, chemical composition, colour and density. In general conversation soils are referred to as *heavy* if they contain a large proportion of clay, *medium* if the balance between fine clay and sand is equal, or *sandy* if the particles are comparatively large permitting free penetration of air and moisture. Soils are further classified as *alkaline* if they contain a measurable proportion of free lime, or *acid* if the reverse is the case and there is a deficiency of calcium. The acidity or alkalinity can be checked by means of a pH test. Colour is frequently influenced by mineral and dead vegetation matter content. Dark soils for example warm up quicker in Spring and look fertile.

All the above facts are of importance because they have a bearing on how the soil needs to be worked for best results and will determine which crops will grow. For example, rhododendrons will only grow on an acid soil.

Soil is not a single substance. It is a mixture of finely ground rock and decaying matter, plant or animal in origin, which breaks down into that tobacco-like substance collectively termed *humus*. Humus has a two-fold effect on the soil: it holds moisture like a sponge and yet helps to keep a clay soil open, allowing air to penetrate freely, so preventing stagnation. Soils, in particular clay, which are short of humus set like a brick in dry weather and are difficult to garden.

A fertile soil contains a thriving population of fungi, bacteria, insects and other life forms. Some are beneficial like the bacteria which live on the roots of garden peas, fixing nitrogen and chemicals essential to plant growth. Others are harmful, as any gardener who has had his cabbages infected with the club

Soil Particles

The illustration (*right*) indicates the different soil particles: (top) sandy soil with large particles, (bottom) clay soil with densely packed particles.

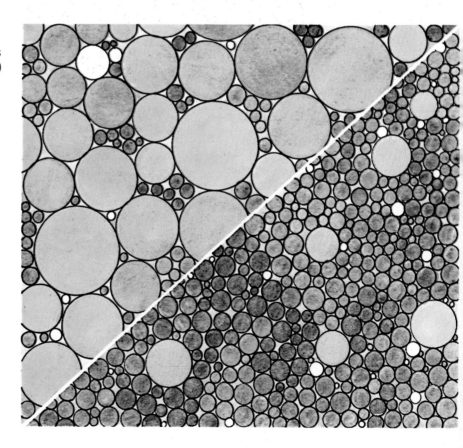

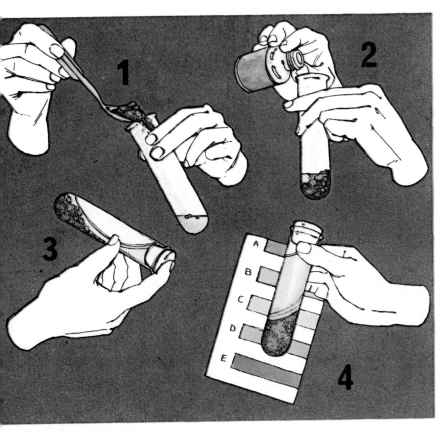

root fungus will appreciate, and some are neutral, maintaining a healthy balance between the others, like the chairman in a political debate on women's rights.

In a well maintained soil supplied with humus and regularly cultivated no problems will arise. But soils can be thrown into an imbalance by the introduction of infected plants, so buy only from an accredited source. Continually growing one crop on the same plot for several years may result in a build up of a particular pest, for example, potato eel worm. Practise a rotation, especially in the kitchen garden, by moving the crops around. Potatoes will not then be grown on the same plot more often than once every four years (see Vegetable chapter page 86 for rotation details).

Bad drainage results in a soil deprived of air, so every effort should be made to correct this by draining, working in all the coarse material available — sand, weathered ash, and organic matter.

How to Make a pH Test.

1 *Take a small sample of soil to be tested, place it in a test tube containing distilled water. Do not handle the soil as this can influence the reading; use a plastic spoon to fill the tube.*

2 *Add some of the special colour indicator which can be purchased from most garden shops.*

3 *Shake it well, using a cork to cover the open end of the tube not the finger.*

4 *The colour left at the top of the tube indicates the pH.* Red *means the soil is acid,* Yellow *is neutral,* green *is alkaline. Intensity of colour is a rough guide to the degree of acidity or alkalinity.*

Illustration right shows a cabbage which has been infected with club root fungus. For details of this and other diseases see chapter on Pests and Diseases, page 116.

Soil Improvements

Clay soils are easily recognised — in wet weather they adhere to boots and spade, and quickly become waterlogged. In dry weather they bake to the hardness of concrete. They are improved by being left rough dug for the Winter because frost breaks up the clay clods into crumbs, by drainage, by dressings of organic matter (anything which will rot to form humus) by mixing in gritty material

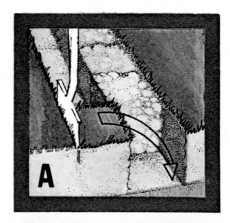

(coarse sand, etc) and, if the material is acid, by a dressing of lime.

Do not work a clay soil when it is excessively wet.

Light soils are improved and increased in fertility by heavy and repeated dressings of organic matter. A mulch of compost, lawn mowings etc, applied to a sandy soil acts as a reservoir of moisture, while the humus layer below stops both water and fertilizer washing straight past the plant roots to be lost in the subsoil.

Digging can mean pricking the soil over with a fork — a desultory exercise after a heavy meal — or the complete inversion of the soil layers 10–20–30 inches (25–50–75 cm) deep.

1. Single Digging as the name implies means turning over the soil to a depth of approximately 10 inches (25 cm) or one spade length (one spit). Take out a trench 12 inches (30 cm) wide by 10 inches (25 cm) deep. Any compost, farm manure, or weeds skimmed from the plot are spread along the trench bottom and covered by the soil as the next trench is opened up (**A**).

2. Double Digging. Take out a trench 18 inches (45 cm) wide and 10 inches (25 cm) deep. Put in the compost or manure but, before covering, get into the trench and break up the trench bottom to the full length of the fork tines, mixing in the compost at the same time (**B**). Open up the next trench and turn the soil over on top of this leaving another trench to be manured then forked (**C**). In this way the soil is improved to a depth of 20 inches (50 cm) and the effect on the crop is remarkable.

Making up a Compost Bin: Make up a container from four posts set out in a square. Fencing rails are nailed to the posts on three sides leaving one inch (2·5 cm) gaps so that the air

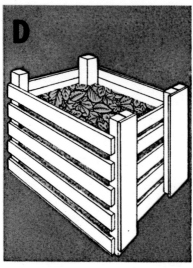

can penetrate (**D**). The open front is closed by a removable panel made in the same way. A sheet of asbestos, roofing felt, or plastic, goes on the top to prevent the heap being soaked by rain.

Building up the Heap: Decay is brought about by the action of bacteria, which function best when supplied with adequate supplies of nitrogen, air and moisture. Grass clippings, cabbage leaves and soft hedge clippings contain sufficient moisture, but dry straw will need wetting to rot down quickly.

Put in first a layer of the material to be composted, then a dusting of nitrogenous activator (there are a number of proprietary brands on the market) then a dusting of soil, followed by another layer of refuse and so on until the bin is full. This sequence is illustrated (**E**) although the activator and soil layers have been exaggerated for identification purposes.

Composting proceeds rapidly in moist humid weather, so will be quicker in Summer, 6 to 8 weeks, slower in Winter, 4 to 6 months. Properly made, the heap should heat sufficiently to kill disease spores, pests, and weed seeds but, to be safe, any questionable material should be excluded.

Make up the heap quickly, making certain the supply of

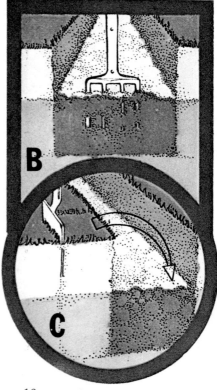

nitrogen, air and moisture is such as to ensure the quickest possible breakdown.

Plant Foods. Farm manure, peat, straw and spent hops may all be used to improve soil texture, depending on their availability.

Organic matter can in some cases be supplemented by direct applications of compound fertilizers, nitrogen, phosphates and potash. The proportion of the three main ingredients is varied according to the way the plot is to be cropped. *Nitrogen* encourages leaf growth so is useful as a pick-me-up for cabbage and spinach where a large tender leaf is the prime requirement. *Phosphates* are needed to encourage healthy root development in young seedlings, or root crops like turnip and beetroot. *Potash* induces a good colour and flavour in fruit, carrots, and celery. A shortage of any one of the three elements has the same effect on the plant as a diet deficiency in human beings; sickness results and unless the correction is made the plant dies.

Lime is a term which covers several materials from ground chalk to quick lime. With nitrogen, phosphates, and potash it is an essential plant food. In the garden, however, lime in some form is more often required as a corrector of acidity. To maintain fertility the gardener dresses the soil with manure or compost. As this breaks down, one of the products is humic acid and in extreme cases if this increases beyond a certain stage plant growth ceases. The only means of correcting this is by dressing the soil with lime.

Lime, then, is essential to plant growth. It has a beneficial physical effect on clay soil by causing the smaller particles to gather into larger crumbs, thus improving drainage and aeration, and is the only means of correcting soil acidity. As a final bonus, lime discourages some fungus diseases such as club-root. Unfortunately, there are other equally important diseases, which thrive in an alkaline soil, which is why soil to be cropped with potatoes is not dressed with lime in any form.

Do not apply lime to soil which has been freshly manured; it causes a loss of available nitrogen. The more clay a soil contains the more lime it needs to correct the acidity.

Because in clay soils the lime is held against being washed out by rain, the dressings are needed less frequently on clay than on light sandy soils.

For example, given a fairly acid condition, sand would need 8 oz of hydrated lime per square yard (200 g/m²) to correct it, whereas clay would need 14 oz per square yard (350 g/m²). To compensate, clay would only need this heavy dressing every four years; sand would need the lighter dressing every two years.

Plant Growth The plant grows by taking up the minerals dissolved in the soil moisture through the fine root hairs. Then by making use of the sun's energy through the medium of chlorophyll, the material which gives leaves or young stems their green colour, it converts relatively simple chemical substances into complex proteins, sugars, and starches.

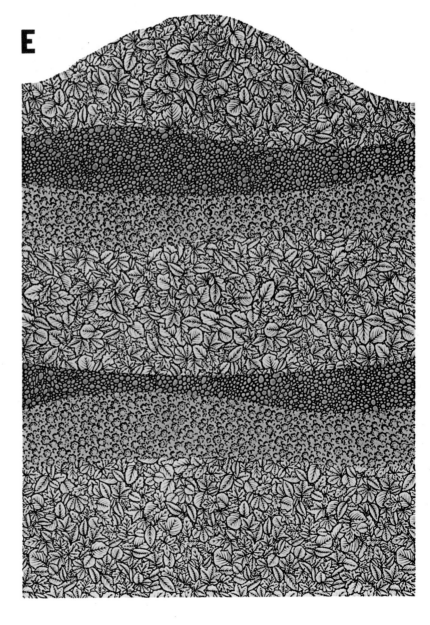

Propagation

The production of new plants either from stock already in the garden, donated by friends, or bought from a nursery is one of the most exciting avenues of gardening to explore.

The seed or sexual means of increasing stock could, I suppose, be described as nature's way. This method is used when the plant in question will breed true to type, or when, by carefully contrived cross pollination, an attempt is being made to produce a new variety. Plants raised from seed are completely new individuals, even though the characteristics may appear identical. Like a human baby, it has resulted from a fusion of two cells, male and female.

Vegetative propagation: A piece of root, branch, or leaf is taken from the desired plant which will grow into an exact replica of the original with all the required characteristics unchanged. Many of the most desirable of our garden plants are increased in this way. Plants raised by any other means than seed are not new but a continuation of the old — all the Michaelmas Daisy 'Ada Ballard' in our gardens are merely extensions of, and the same age as, the original.

Equipment

When raising plants from seed a certain amount of basic equipment is necessary to begin with. Other items can be added as the need arises.

Seed pans, either clay or plastic, 5 inches (13 cm) in diameter are a useful size for sowing seed into, with standard seed trays to prick off the seedlings from the pans when they require more space.

A heated frame or greenhouse is of considerable help when raising large quantities of seedlings, as the gardener may then maintain the best growing conditions. Failing this, the kitchen or bathroom window ledge may be commandeered for a week or two each Spring. The large trays with a clear polythene top are useful for this type of indoor gardening.

Composts are now simplified — a standard mixture can be obtained or made up to a recipe which will suit the average gardener's needs. Those formulated by the John Innes Institute, provided they are made from the recommended ingredients, are quite adequate for the plants commonly cultivated in the majority of gardens.

A mixture known as John Innes No 1 compost will suit seedlings pricked out from the seed compost. Plants which require a richer diet should have twice the fertilizer added to the basic mixture John Innes No 2, or 3 times the fertilizer John Innes No 3.

With good quality soil (loam) becoming increasingly difficult to obtain some modern composts are now based on peat. Soil is omitted altogether. The quality is consistent, it is clean to handle, and the same mixture can be used from seed stage to maturity if supple-

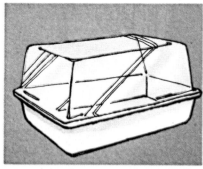

mentary feeding is attended to. The basic equipment necessary to raise plants from seed can be selected from the following:
Top left. A tray with polythene top suitable for indoor propagation
Bottom left. Clay or plastic seed pans for sowing seed indoors
Top right. Seed tray for pricking off seedlings
Bottom right. A heated frame for raising seedlings under ideal growing conditions.
It is well within the capabilities of the handyman-gardener to make his own frames and seed boxes, and even small propagation units which fit comfortably on a living room window sill.
Frames and cloches, to be really useful in the garden, should be light enough to be moved easily from one point to another for the various crops that are going to be grown in them.

Seed Sowing

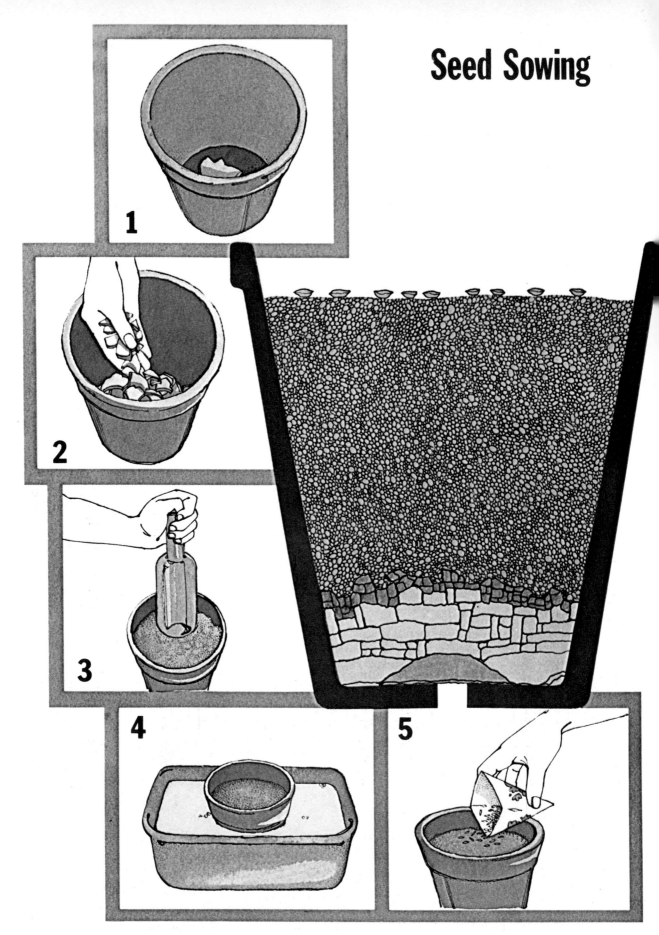

Seed sowing is simple provided certain basic rules are observed. The seed needs moisture, warmth, air, and sowing at the correct depth.

Large seeds may be sown individually spaced at $\frac{1}{4}$ to $\frac{1}{2}$ inch (6–12 mm) apart.

Fine seeds like begonia or lobelia may be mixed with brick dust or dry fine sand — a simple method of ensuring even distribution. Brick dust is obtained by crushing weathered brick with a large hammer.

Correct depth of sowing is important.

Very fine seed is best not covered at all, just firmed into the compost with a pot press. Larger seed will need no more covering than their own depth of compost.

1 Take a clean pot, cover the drainage hole at the base with a piece of broken clay plant pot or perforated zinc.

2 On top of this put more broken pot graded to an average quarter inch (6 mm) size; a small amount of roughage, the material which just failed to pass the $\frac{3}{8}$ inch (1 cm) riddle will do, or a layer of peat. This stops the fine material washing through to block the drainage.

3 The compost goes on top of this and is firmed down to within half an inch (13 mm) of the rim with a pot press. A press can be made to fit the pot

from any smooth surfaced object. A tobacco tin, a piece of wood, or even a bottle is effective.

4 Plunge the pots in a bowl of water until the compost is evenly soaked right through.

5 Then sow the seed evenly across the surface of the compost. Seed must always be sown thinly. Overcrowded seedlings are drawn, weak and at risk from disease.

6 Cover seed pans and pots with a sheet of glass to conserve moisture and newspaper which prevents scorching. Complete darkness assists germination in some seeds. The paper must be removed immediately the seedlings appear.

Some seed which shows a reluctance to germinate will frequently do so if given a temperature below freezing for a few days after sowing. Molucella, bells of Ireland, gentian, and primula are examples.

Rose hips, hollyberries and similar fruit, if placed in a pot between layers of sand in a container which is left outdoors for 12 months, will grow away strongly the following Spring. A covering of perforated zinc is advisable to stop mice eating the whole lot.

7 Once germinated, seedlings must be thinned or pricked off, and kept in full light to ensure strong sturdy growth. An

even temperature will also be of help.

It is vital, once the seedlings have been pricked off, to ensure that they grow away without any check at all. This means that at all times there is adequate moisture. Humid growing conditions are essential to achieve the sort of progress that will ensure you have a healthy plant to go out into the open ground. Because the cost of raising plants from seed is relatively cheap, compared with buying-in mature specimens, it is possible to experiment. Do not be restricted to the 'run of the mill' things. Do not stick to Antirrhinum — explore the more interesting field of unusual plants, and it is astonishing how this increase in variety will add to the hobby of gardening as a whole.

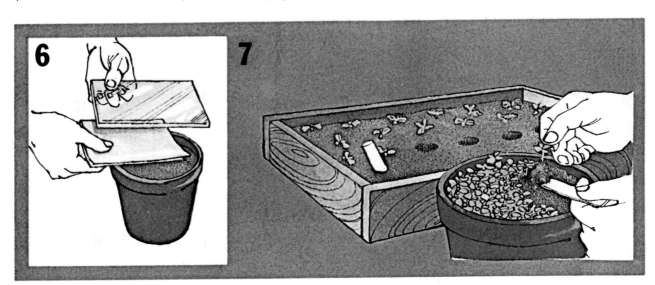

Cuttings

There are many methods by which plants may be increased in quantity other than seed.

Cuttings, layers, division, budding, and grafting all have a place in the gardener's repertoire, all, unlike seed, are non-sexual.

Cuttings may be made from any part of the plant which can be separated from the parent, and persuaded to root, then grown to maturity.

Stem Cuttings are further classified according to their condition at the time of removal into *soft*, those taken early in the growing season; *semi hardwood* or half ripe cuttings made from shoots just beginning to harden at the base; or *hardwood* which are made from mature one-year-old growth at the end of the season.

The rooting conditions are important. A closed frame over a bed of 2 parts sharp lime-free sand and 1 part peat is a good standard mixture, and with underheating would be ideal.

Soft Wood Cuttings (1): particularly prone to dehydration so are usually short jointed; up to 4 inches (10 cm) long removed with a sharp knife, stripped of the lower leaves, dipped in a suitable rooting powder, then inserted for approximately one third its length in the rooting medium. Care must be made to ensure they never dry out which is why a closed frame helps. For small quantities the cuttings may be inserted around the rim of a clay pot, using the sand/peat mixture, then enclosed in a polythene bag which is then sealed until the cuttings have rooted. Make sure the cuttings are firmed well into the compost — slack planting means air spaces, drying out and in consequence poor rooting.

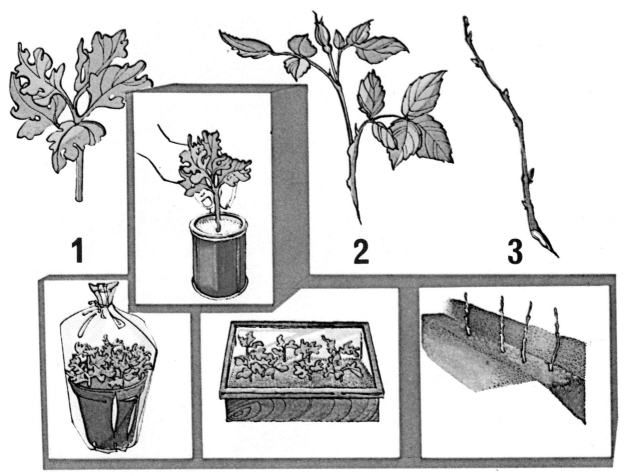

1 **2** **3**

Semi Hardwood Cuttings (2): less prone to drying out than soft wood, but must still be kept in a close humid atmosphere; a frame with underheating provides this. The cutting is usually taken below a leaf joint or with a sliver of old wood attached, known as a heel. Otherwise, treatment is as for soft material, though rooting may take slightly longer. This type is usually available for taking halfway through the growing season.

Hardwood Cuttings (3): taken just as the plants go into resting or dormant period. Again they are cut below a leaf joint or with a heel of old wood and are of current season's growth. Because the wood is fully ripe they are not so vulnerable to drying out. They may be rooted outdoors in a sandy soil or in a cold frame. As a rule hardwood cuttings are considerably longer than any of the others described.

Outdoors, make a straight backed trench 5 inches (13 cm) deep on a sheltered border. Put a 2 inch (5 cm) layer of coarse sand in the bottom and insert the cuttings into this, firm in with the feet to prevent frost loosening them over winter.

Leaf Cuttings are an interesting method of propagation for Ramonda, Haberlea, and many house plants notably African violets and begonia. Choose leaves which are healthy, vigorous and just approaching full development. Remove the leaf

plus a length of stalk and insert into a compost of 3 parts sharp sand and 1 part peat. The lower portion of the leaf should be in firm contact with the compost, **B**.

Begonia leaves can be persuaded to produce 6–12 plantlets per leaf if the main veins on the leaf back are slit with a razor blade, and the whole leaf pegged flat onto the compost with stubbing wire, **A**. A closed frame or polythene bag provides the correct humid atmosphere.

Root Cuttings are also taken during the Autumn, and are so easy to make it is a pity only some plants will respond. Acanthus, phlox, and certain euphorbias are just a few examples, but any plant with fairly thick roots would be worth trying.

Cut the roots into sections about 2 inches (5 cm) long, square cut at the top, slanting at the bottom, and insert them in a sandy compost. The tops of the cuttings are just covered with the compost. Buds will have

formed and growth commenced by the following Spring, **C**.

Bud Cuttings, Layering and Division

1   2   3

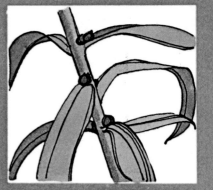

1

2

3

Bud Cuttings (far left)

1 Cut a section of a young stem carrying a leaf with a bud at its base.

2 Cut the stem section all the way down the middle.

3 Bury the stem section horizontally in the compost, leaf uppermost, with the bud just showing.

Cormlets (upper left)

Many bulbs, like gladiolus, spawn by developing cormlets around the base. Picked off and sown like seed, they grow to flowering size in about two years.

Bulbils (left)

Lilies produce bulbils at the axils of the leaves which, when picked off and set 8 to 10 in a seed pan, will grow into new plants.

Ground Layering (left)

From the parent plant choose a conveniently placed shoot, cut into or slit the lower side of the stem without severing it, treat with rooting powder and peg down into sandy compost. A heavy stone or brick will prevent the stem from rising. Roots will form where the stem was cut.

Air Layering (far left)

1 Near the tip of a young branch slice into the stem for about 1½ inches (4 cm) and dust with rooting powder.

2 Insert sphagnum moss into the cut to hold it open.

3 Pack wet sphagnum moss around the cut and enclose in a polythene bag, tightly sealed at each end, through which root development can be checked. When enough root has been formed, cut the branch off and pot.

Bud or Eye cuttings, as used for vines and camellia, consist of clipping a young stem into sections each carrying a leaf with a bud at its base. Bury the stem and leaf base so the bud is just showing through the compost, and roots will soon form.

Many bulbs are increased by spawn, the cormlets from around gladioli are an example. Sown like seed they will grow to flowering size in about 2 years.

Lilies produce bulbils in the leaf axils; these can be planted up 8 or 10 to a seed pan. Lilies may also be propagated by removing a quantity of the broad fleshy scales of which the bulb is composed, mixing them with peat and sand in a polythene bag, then hanging it up in the airing cupboard. Roots and shoots are quickly developed at which time the scales are potted up individually.

Layering consists of pulling a conveniently placed shoot of the plant it is desired to propagate down to soil level. The under surface is slit or twisted in some way, treated with rooting powder, then pegged into a sandy compost, and while still attached to the parent plant induced to form roots. A heavy stone placed on the stem or a long wooden peg ensure the branch is held firm until rooting takes place.

Air Layering. Select a young branch, make a slit in the centre towards the tip, about 1½ inches (4 cm) long. Dust it with rooting powder, insert a wisp of sphagnum moss to hold the cut open, pack it around with more wet sphagnum moss, then enclose the whole lot in a polythene bag sealed at each end with tape.

Root growth can be checked through the bag, and when forward enough the branch is severed and potted up.

Division. As the name implies this consists of pieces pulled from a parent plant with shoots and roots already formed, a method used when propagating herbaceous plants. Two forks pushed into the plant back to back, then levered apart, will usually persuade even the stubbornest paeonia to be pulled apart. Use the young outer portions of plants like michaelmas daisy discarding the old woody central portion.

Sand, the rooting medium for most cuttings, has no nutrient in it whatsoever so once cuttings have rooted and are growing away they must be moved into a medium which provides them with a balanced diet. Either the John Innes compost or one of the composts based on peat will be quite suitable.

Division

1 To divide herbaceous plants, insert two forks back to back into the plant and lever apart.

2 Sub-divide into smaller sections ready for planting out.

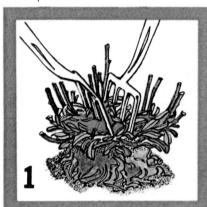

Grafting

Grafting is a technique used for producing fruit trees and also many of our ornamental trees, for example, hybrid rhododendrons; indeed any plant which is difficult to propagate by other means. A young shoot, known as the scion, of the variety it is desired to propagate is joined to the root of another, termed the stock. Grafting is usually done just as growth starts in Spring, the stock being just a little further advanced in growth than the scion. The plants must be closely enough related for a union to form, and the cut surface must be so aligned that the actively growing areas can unite. They are then bound firmly together and the whole is made watertight with grafting wax. Cuts must be smooth and clean and never allowed to dry out.

There are many different forms of grafting: whip and tongue, saddle, and rind grafting, are the methods most commonly used.

Budding is another method of grafting, the difference being in this case that the scion to be joined consists of a single bud, and it is inserted in the middle of the growing season. Most H.T. and floribunda roses are propagated by budding.

Buds are cut from young shoots, usually the mid portion of the stem. They should be squat, plump and firm. Unripened tips are of no use. Stocks should be young, so the bark is pliable and parts easily from the wood. If the bark lifts freely bud insertion is much easier. Make a 'T' shaped incision in the root stock. Cut a bud complete with shield of bark from the stem or bud stock by inserting the knife half an inch (13 mm) below the bud and coming out the same dis-

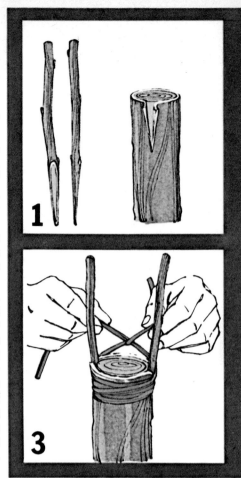

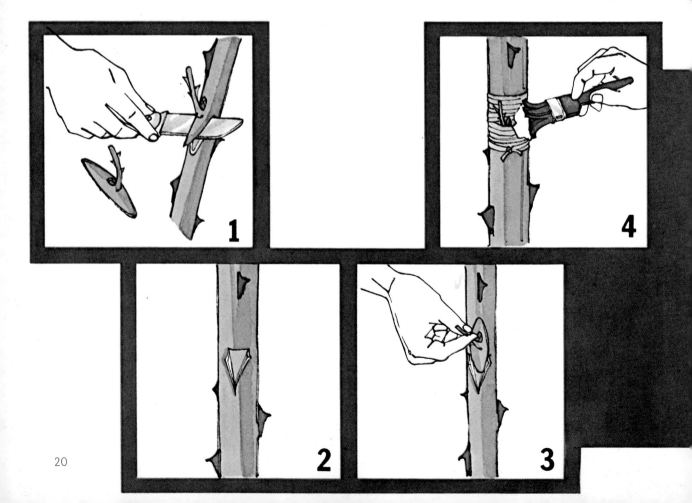

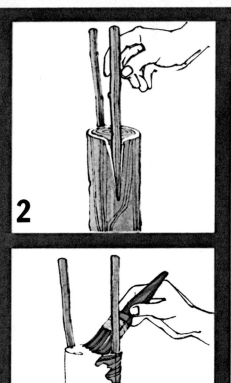

Rind Graft *(left)*

1 Square cut a stem of the root stock and make two vertical cuts in its bark; cut the ends of two scion cuttings.

2 Place sliced ends of scion cuttings in the vertical cuts in the stock.

3 Bind with tape to secure firmly in position.

4 Coat the joint completely with grafting wax to seal it.

Saddle Graft *(top right)*

Double cut the stem of the root stock into a wedge shape; cut into the scion so that it fits closely on to the stock; bind and seal with grafting wax.

Whip and Tongue Graft *(right)*

Cut the ends of the root stock and the scion cutting as shown.

Standard Rose Budding *(left)*

1 About ½ inch (13 mm) below the bud on the scion slice into the stem (to not more than half the thickness) and finish ½ inch (13 mm) above the bud.

2 Make a T-shaped cut in the stem of the root stock and open the bark.

3 Using the leaf stalk as a handle, push the bud shank into the T-shaped cut under the bark; cut back the shank above the bud to fit square into the top of the T.

4 Bind firmly and seal

tance above, finishing with a tearing motion. Do not penetrate too deeply into the stem on this cut, certainly not more than half way. Leave the leaf stalk to act as a handle. Push the bud into the 'T' shaped cut of the root stock, using the knife handle to open the bark. Trim the top square so it fits snugly into the 'T' cross piece, then tie firmly into position. Check to see the bud remains plump and make certain every few weeks the tie is not too tight.

H.T. and floribunda roses are budded as near the root as possible.

Fruit trees bush — 12 inches (30 cm) above ground.

Fruit trees, half standards or standards — 2 ft (60 cm) up to 6 ft (182 cm) above ground level.

Standard roses are worked on to wild dog rose (*Rosa canina*) or Japanese rose (*R. rugosa*). With the canina stock old stems are headed back to a height of between 3½–5 ft (1·10–1·50 m).

The following Spring each stem is restricted to three young shoots near the top and evenly spaced to form a balanced head. All other shoots are rubbed out. In mid Summer a bud is inserted near the base of each young shoot.

When R. rugosa is used as the stock the buds are inserted direct into the main stem at the height required.

The root stocks for any form of budding or grafting must be selected for vigour, health, and all round adaptability. Line them out in land which has been deeply worked and is free from perennial weeds.

Stocks for grafting are planted in Autumn, then budded the second Spring after planting.

Stocks for bud working are planted in late Autumn/early Winter for budding during the following Summer.

Some plants produce what are termed suckers which can be removed and transplanted as required.

Roses

The rose is really the pack horse of the gardening world. Sometimes the burden it is asked to carry in regard to soil and situation is intolerable. Roses will grow in almost every country in the world, adapt to nearly every condition of soil and exposure, but they respond as few other flowering shrubs will to careful cultivation.

A deeply worked, moisture-retentive soil with a reasonable proportion of clay is ideal. The heavier clays need lightening with dressings of organic matter and weathered ash or similar inert material. Conversely the light sands need to be made moisture-retentive with organic matter, both dug into the soil before planting, and as a mulch during the Summer.

Choose the sunniest, most open site available. Roses will tolerate shade for part of the day only. Free movement of air reduces the risk of fungal attack, in particular mildew, and to some extent greenfly. Over zealous protection of roses is a mistake frequently made, as is the over crowding of the bushes within the confines of the bed.

This does not mean roses enjoy a draughty position; there are few plants which will tolerate for example the shaded, damp wind tunnel between two houses. Places like this are to be avoided at all costs.

Prepare the soil in the Autumn ready for planting the bushes in Spring. Clay soil must be worked to a depth of 20 inches (50 cm) to ensure drainage is not impeded in any way. Wet soils inhibit root development which means weak unhealthy growth.

Roses prefer a soil which is slightly acid. Heavy feeding will tend to increase this acidity so make regular pH tests and apply lime to the beds as required.

To make good the 3–4 feet (1·0–1·25 m) of growth which is removed annually, and to produce flowers continuously for about five months, the bushes need a soil well supplied with food. Build up the fertility before planting and maintain it during the life of the bed by regular feeding and mulching.

Frequently standard roses are planted in a lawn or narrow border. Prepare the holes to re-

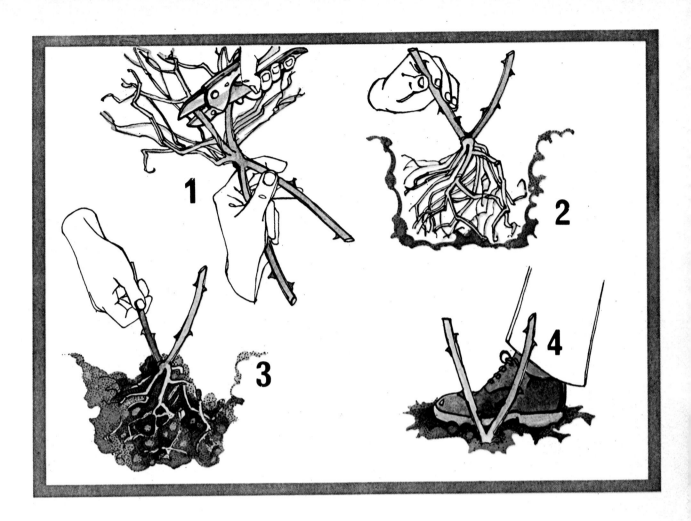

ceive them in advance, two spades deep, and half as wide again as the root spread. Badly prepared holes, especially on heavy land, just gather water and would be more suitable to growing tadpoles than roses.

The nurseries despatch the rose bushes at any time between mid Autumn and early Spring. Should they arrive before the bed is ready, or when the weather is unsuitable for planting, 'lay them in' by taking out a trench on a sheltered side. Bury the roots so the stems are held at an angle of 45 degrees until conditions are right for planting.

Remember that roots are active long before there is any sign of top growth, so do not delay too long. Late planting means a serious check to growth early in the life of the rose.

Before Planting

1 Trim the roots. I trim all roots back when planting roses to encourage the fibrous root formation which establishes quickly in their new quarters.

2 Make sure the hole provided is large enough to take the roots comfortably.

3 The depth of the hole is adjusted so that the base of the branches (point of budding) is approximately $1-1\frac{1}{2}$ inches (25–38 mm) below the soil level when planting is complete. Standards, of course, are adjusted for depth according to the soil mark on the stem. To ensure all the roots are in intimate contact with the soil lift the bush up and down as the hole is filled, this works the soil in between the roots.

4 Tread the soil firm except the top 2 inches (5 cm) which are left loose.

Standard and weeping standard roses must be staked then tied in immediately after planting. Settling of the soil may take place leaving the budding point exposed. The level may be restored by top dressing or mulching.

Container growing means that bedding roses can be planted at any time when soil conditions permit. Do not disturb the root ball when the container is removed.

Watering and liquid feeding, to establish the plant quickly, is particularly important in early and mid Summer.

Prune harder than is usual the following Spring so that the bush can be shaped.

Pruning

Newly planted roses are cut back hard leaving only two or three buds above soil level. The best time to prune all bedding roses both new and established is early to mid Spring, depending on the weather conditions.

Hard pruning of newly planted bushes encourages strong root action, and in consequence vigorous top growth.

Pruning of established roses depends very much on the variety and should aim at concentrating the plant's energy into the formation of strong, healthy young wood capable of maximum flowering.

Firstly, remove dead or damaged shoots and useless thin or crossing wood. Then bearing in mind the character of the variety, prune the remaining shoots to an outward facing bud. Cuts should be made close enough to a bud so there is no die back, yet not so close as to damage the growing point (*see illustration*).

Strong growing varieties, for example 'Peace' or 'Wendy Cussons', are pruned less severely than weaker specimens such as 'Franklin Engelmann' or 'Troika'.

On all bushes the weaker shoots are pruned harder than the more vigorous growths. Hard pruning stimulates greater effort and balances up the bush. *Strong Growers:* prune to 9 buds on vigorous shoots, 6 buds on the weak growths.
Weak Growers: prune to 6 buds on strong shoots, 3 buds on the weak.

Never allow a cluster of dead shoots to build up at soil level. Cut all dead tissue away as it just forms a source of infection for disease organisms.

Standard Roses

Adjust the pruning so as to form a symmetrical head. Careful pruning prevents the one sided heads which result from careless budding. Thin out twiggy or unwanted shoots and cut back the remainder by half their length.

Rambler Roses

Rambler roses which only produce one flush of flowers may be pruned when blossoming is over. Indeed, the sooner the old shoots which have flowered are cut away the better so the young shoots to supply the display the following year can be tied in to replace them.

The pruning and training of climbing roses is important. Removal of old wood must be balanced according to the amount of new wood that is available to take its place. Train the new shoots along the wall horizontally rather than up the wall vertically. Pulling shoots down restricts the sap stream and encourages the branch to side shoot along its whole length. When branches are allowed to grow vertically they often become bare of shoots at the base. When little or no new wood is being produced, cutting old worn-out wood right out to the base will often stimulate dormant buds to break and grow strong young shoots. Side buds on the established framework are cut back to two or three buds.

Shrub Roses

Shrub roses need only dead heading, removal of twiggy superfluous shoots, and general shaping of the bush. When young wood is required, cut selected shoots right out to the base.

Feeding

All roses need feeding but particularly the H.T. and floribunda which are pruned heavily each year. Apply a general fertilizer dressing at 2 oz per square yard (70 g/m²) as growth commences in Spring. Mulch the soil with rotted manure, compost, peat, or similar material immediately afterwards. A further feed of complete fertilizer at 2 oz per square yard, (70 g/m²), well watered in after the first flush of flowers, should provide all basic requirements.

Two sprays overhead with 1 oz of Epsom salts dissolved in a gallon (30 g in 4·5 litres) of water per 24 roses takes care of the roses' high demand for magnesium.

Supplementary feeding as a liquid can be adjusted according

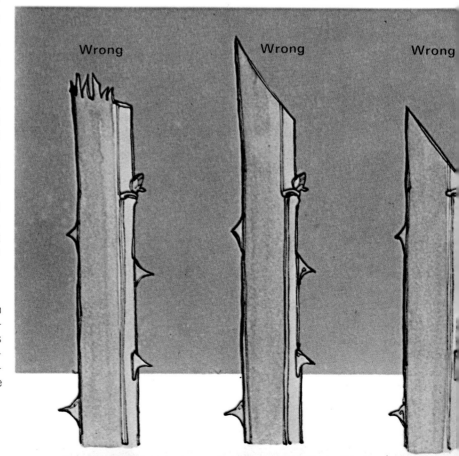

Wrong   Wrong   Wrong

to the season or individual plant's need. Growth must be allowed to harden down before Winter as soft growth is liable to be killed by the frost.

Clean out weeds as they appear, onto the compost heap. Remove any suckers by clearing away the soil and pulling them out as close to the main stem as possible. One of the *Paraquat* based weed killers can be used to clear both weeds and suckers.

Summer Pruning
As the flowers fade they should be removed to make way for a second or third crop.

Autumn Pruning
Cut back long top growths by approximately one third their length in late Autumn to prevent the bushes being rocked loose by the wind.

Pest and Disease Control
Good cultivation and garden hygiene help a lot in keeping the problem of pests and disease to a minimum. Greenfly (*illustrated right*) can be a problem some years, but are easily controlled

by one of the systemic insecticides, which are absorbed into the sap stream of the plant. Saw fly, capsid, thrip, and frog hoppers will all succumb to the systemic spray, or Derris pyrethrum, lindane, malathion.

Diseases
Choose rose varieties which are not disease prone. 'Frensham', for example, will develop mildew irrespective of prevailing soil and weather conditions, whereas 'Evelyn Fison' exhibits a remarkable resistance to mildew and blackspot.

There are now systemic fungicides available which, if used according to instructions, will keep the disease under control.

The appearance of rust coincides with fluctuating soil moisture. Keep the soil evenly wet by watering and mulching.

Collect and burn all fallen leaves or prunings to make sure over-wintering fungal spores are destroyed. A winter wash with a

sulphur based fungicide in late Winter is also an advantage.

Propagation
Commercially, roses are propagated by budding. This technique is described in the chapter on propagation (*page 20*).

What is not so well known is that almost all roses, including H.T. and Floribunda, will root readily from semi-hardwood or hardwood cuttings.

Semi-hardwood cuttings are best made from shoots which have just flowered, taken with a heel of old wood or immediately under a leaf joint. The cuttings are dipped first in rooting powder, then inserted into a compost of sharp sand and peat.

Hardwood cuttings are made in the same manner in mid Autumn, but will root inserted in light sandy soil outdoors. Because the shoots are fully ripened they can be much longer but there is no real advantage in this.

Right

Varieties

12 H.T. Suitable for General Cultivation

'Alec's Red': Cherry red, no scent. 30–36 inches (75–90 cm).

'Beauté': Buff and light orange, slightly fragrant. 30 inches (75 cm). Useful as cut flower because of unusual colour.

'E. H. Morse': Rich red, sweetly scented. Dark, disease free foliage. Approx. 36 inches (90 cm).

'Grandpa Dickson': Flower opens yellow fading to cream. Disease-resistent foliage. Upright strong growth up to 40 inches (1·0 m).

'Mullard Jubilee': The deep rose pink flowers are fragrant and carried several to a head. Vigorous, well furnished growth up to 30 inches (75 cm). Good display.

'Northern Lights': A beautifully formed rose with a tendency on some soils to deteriorate in quality on the second flush of blossom. Canary yellow petals, flushed pink. Moderately fragrant.

'Peace': The best known of all H.T. roses and splendid value. Extremely vigorous up to 48 inches (1·2 m) with deep green disease-resistant foliage. Prune lightly or some of the shoots fail to flower. Yellow flushed pink.

'Piccadilly': A fragrant bi-colour, scarlet with a pale yellow reverse. Excellent for planting where there is partial shade from the mid-day sun. 30 inches (75 cm).

'Sutter's Gold': Worth growing for the fragrance of the orange flowers alone. A good, weather-resistant bedding rose. 30 inches (75 cm).

'Rose Gaujard': Creamy white petals flushed with carmine. Ideal for garden display. Strong glossy disease-resistant growth. Up to 36 inches (90 cm).

'Wendy Cussons': Cerise scarlet and very fragrant. Good either for bedding, or budded as a standard. Dark, glossy, disease-resistant foliage. 36 inches (90 cm).

'Whisky Mac': Flowers a mixture of gold, bronze and tangerine. Strong, disease-resistant foliage. 30 inches (75 cm).

12 Floribunda Roses for General Planting

'All Gold': Compact growth up to 24 inches (60 cm). Semi-double buttercup yellow flowers, slightly fragrant. Fairly disease-resistant but may be prone to black spot on some soils.

'Blessings': A good bedding rose, sometimes listed as H.T. but exhibits a floribunda character. Soft coral pink, fragrant. 36 inches (90 cm).

'Busy Lizzie': Compact growth up to 24 inches (60 cm). Pink flowers are borne in large trusses over a long period. Looks well in association with 'All Gold'.

'City of Leeds': Even though the flowers mark in wet weather this is a quality bedding rose. Dark green foliage shows the salmon red flowers to full

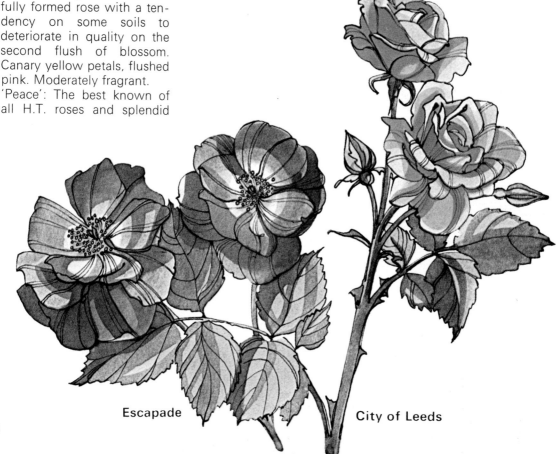

Escapade   City of Leeds

advantage. 36 inches (90 cm).

'Elizabeth of Glamis': Salmon pink hardly describes the flower colour which at times carries an apricot undertone. The large full double flowers are delightfully scented. Height 36 inches (90 cm) but it objects to being planted in badly drained, cold soils.

'Escapade': Rosy magenta flowers — not a colour which suits every taste. The trusses are carried over a long period and have a fragrance reminiscent of the old musk rose. 30 inches (75 cm). Disease-resistant foliage.

'Evelyn Fison': One of the top six bedding roses. Neat compact growth up to 28 inches (70 cm). Brilliant red flowers, slightly fragrant, are carried throughout the Summer. Disease-resistant.

'Icewhite': Vigorous growth up to 48 inches (1·2 m) with a tendency to develop mildew late in the season. An outstanding bedding rose, the white flushed pink flowers are carried in large trusses.

Lightly pruned will make a useful hedge.

'Kerryman': Included here because, as with 'Blessings', it looks more like a Floribunda, with H.T-like flowers in clustered heads. Officially it should be included with the H.T. The flowers are a blend of superlative pink. Growth robust but compact up to 24 inches (60 cm). Disease resistance good.

'Marlena': A neat bedding rose 18 inches (45 cm) high. Suitable for small gardens. Crimson scarlet, semi-double flowers in multi-headed clusters.

'Orange Sensation': One of the best bedding roses. The light vermillion blooms are carried over several months and are scented. Height 24 inches (60 cm).

'Picasso': The blossoms are two shades of red, curiously painted with streaks and flecks of white. This, combined with a long flowering season and freedom from disease, makes this an interesting bedding rose.

Pillar Climbing Roses

'Casino': Good deep yellow. Glossy green foliage. Repeat flowering.

'Danse du Feu': Coral red blooms right through the season. Shiny deep green foliage.

'Shot Silk': Cerise pink petals shaded salmon are produced on strong vigorous shoots. Very fragrant.

'Pink Perpetue': Bright rose pink blooms. Free flowering over a long season.

'Maigold': Bronze yellow double flowers, glossy green attractive foliage, vigorous growth.

'Schoolgirl': Beautifully formed H.T. type flowers, coppery pink, slightly fragrant. Moderately vigorous.

Ramblers

'Albertine': Soft salmon pink flowers. Vigorous growth.

'Crimson Shower': Semi-double crimson flowers in clusters over two or three months.

'New Dawn': Soft pink, perpetual flowering. Vigorous growth.

Beauté

Alec's Red

Schoolgirl

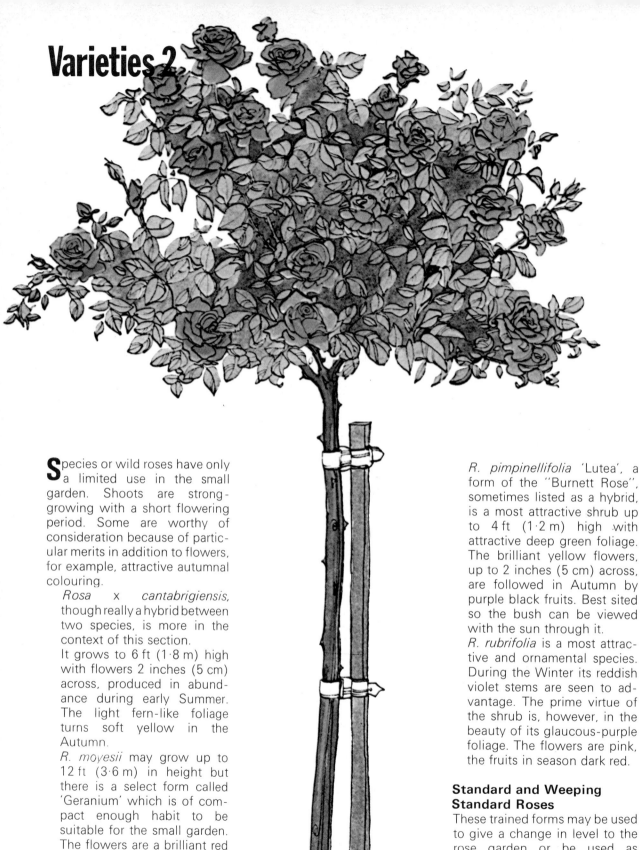

Varieties 2

Species or wild roses have only a limited use in the small garden. Shoots are strong-growing with a short flowering period. Some are worthy of consideration because of particular merits in addition to flowers, for example, attractive autumnal colouring.

Rosa x cantabrigiensis, though really a hybrid between two species, is more in the context of this section.

It grows to 6 ft (1·8 m) high with flowers 2 inches (5 cm) across, produced in abundance during early Summer. The light fern-like foliage turns soft yellow in the Autumn.

R. moyesii may grow up to 12 ft (3·6 m) in height but there is a select form called 'Geranium' which is of compact enough habit to be suitable for the small garden. The flowers are a brilliant red which gain by contrast with the lustrous green foliage. Hips which ripen in late Summer are 2–3 inches (5–7 cm) long.

R. pimpinellifolia 'Lutea', a form of the "Burnett Rose", sometimes listed as a hybrid, is a most attractive shrub up to 4 ft (1·2 m) high with attractive deep green foliage. The brilliant yellow flowers, up to 2 inches (5 cm) across, are followed in Autumn by purple black fruits. Best sited so the bush can be viewed with the sun through it.

R. rubrifolia is a most attractive and ornamental species. During the Winter its reddish violet stems are seen to advantage. The prime virtue of the shrub is, however, in the beauty of its glaucous-purple foliage. The flowers are pink, the fruits in season dark red.

Standard and Weeping Standard Roses

These trained forms may be used to give a change in level to the rose garden or be used as specimen plantings in a patio garden.

Standard roses which are generally H.T. or Floribunda varieties require no particular

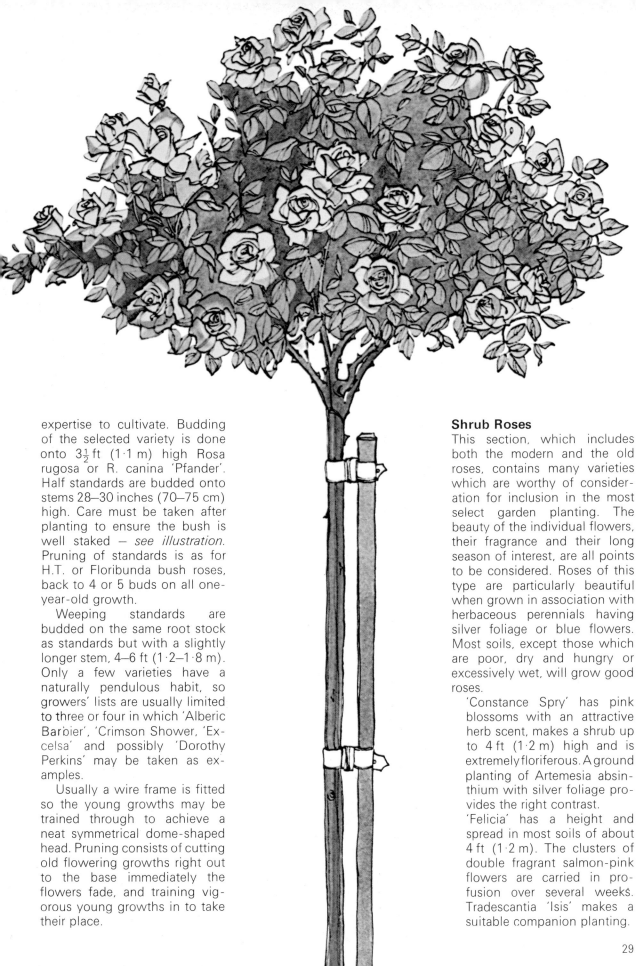

expertise to cultivate. Budding of the selected variety is done onto $3\frac{1}{2}$ ft (1·1 m) high Rosa rugosa or R. canina 'Pfander'. Half standards are budded onto stems 28–30 inches (70–75 cm) high. Care must be taken after planting to ensure the bush is well staked – *see illustration*. Pruning of standards is as for H.T. or Floribunda bush roses, back to 4 or 5 buds on all one-year-old growth.

Weeping standards are budded on the same root stock as standards but with a slightly longer stem, 4–6 ft (1·2–1·8 m). Only a few varieties have a naturally pendulous habit, so growers' lists are usually limited to three or four in which 'Alberic Barbier', 'Crimson Shower, 'Excelsa' and possibly 'Dorothy Perkins' may be taken as examples.

Usually a wire frame is fitted so the young growths may be trained through to achieve a neat symmetrical dome-shaped head. Pruning consists of cutting old flowering growths right out to the base immediately the flowers fade, and training vigorous young growths in to take their place.

Shrub Roses

This section, which includes both the modern and the old roses, contains many varieties which are worthy of consideration for inclusion in the most select garden planting. The beauty of the individual flowers, their fragrance and their long season of interest, are all points to be considered. Roses of this type are particularly beautiful when grown in association with herbaceous perennials having silver foliage or blue flowers. Most soils, except those which are poor, dry and hungry or excessively wet, will grow good roses.

'Constance Spry' has pink blossoms with an attractive herb scent, makes a shrub up to 4 ft (1·2 m) high and is extremely floriferous. A ground planting of Artemesia absinthium with silver foliage provides the right contrast.

'Felicia' has a height and spread in most soils of about 4 ft (1·2 m). The clusters of double fragrant salmon-pink flowers are carried in profusion over several weeks. Tradescantia 'Isis' makes a suitable companion planting.

Varieties 3
Shrub Roses – continued

'Fritz Nobis' grows into an arching branched bush 4–5 ft (1·2–1·5 m) high by as much across and is in the front rank of modern shrub roses. The clove-scented salmon-pink flowers appear throughout Summer. A beautiful effect is achieved when this shrub is grown grouped with Rosa rubrifolia or the "Venetian Sumach", Cotinus cog gy-gria 'Royal Purple'.

'Frühlingsgold' is rather tall-growing for inclusion in the smaller garden but is out-standingly lovely when the long arching stems are fes-tooned with pale yellow semi-double scented blooms. Blue flowered iris make a splendid contrast.

'Golden Chersonese' develops a thicket of interlacing branches which become a mass of single deep golden flowers in late Spring. Height 4 ft (1·2 m) by 3 ft (90 cm) spread. Omphalodes verna, the "Creeping Forget-me-not", with intense blue flowers is a suitable ground cover.

'Roseraie de l'Hay' grows vigorously in all but the most exposed positions up to 4–5 ft (1·2–1·5 m) in height. The large double purple-crimson flowers open in maturity to show creamy yellow stamens. The annual Limnanthes doug-lasii with cream and yellow flowers will, by contrast, ac-centuate the rich colouring of the rose.

Roses, because of their long flowering season, their adaptability over the widest range of soils and their labour-saving character, are the most popular of all garden plants. They can be had in perfection of flower as illustrated by 'Teenager' or in profusion of flower as illustrated in 'All Gold'. You can get them for bedding, for growing on trellises, or for growing in borders in conjunction with herbaceous plants.

The fertility of the rose ensures that its popularity will continue. In addition, the wide range of flower colour and shape, and its usefulness as a cut flower, makes it unequalled by any other flowering plant.

Lawns

A good lawn can only be achieved by giving the grass similar care to that which is lavished on the vegetable or flower garden.

No amount of feeding or after care will compensate for neglecting any of the preliminary cultivations. Many of the faults which develop in a lawn in later years can be traced to incomplete initial cultivations.

Make certain the drainage is good enough to take away surplus moisture. Waterlogging brings all sorts of problems with disease, and makes it almost impossible to grow the fine-leaved desirable grasses. Mowing a lawn which turns into a bog after every rain shower is a source of constant irritation.

Drains may be laid to a soak-away in the lowest corner of the garden. Dig the hole for making the soak-away 3 or 4 ft (1·0– 1·3 m) deep by as much wide. Lead the drainage pipes into this, then fill it to within 12 inches (30 cm) of the surface with broken stones. A topping of quarter inch (6 mm) gravel and the soak-away is transformed into a useful sitting out area, so nothing is wasted (*see below left*).

When changes in level require moving large quantities of soil, it is often easier to import extra soil to even up the surface. Failing this, remove the top soil (**1**) and do the levelling by moving the sub soil (**2**), then replace the fertile top soil to the same depth as it was previously (**3**) over the area to be grassed down.

Heavy soils may be improved with dressings of sand, wea-thered ashes or similar inert material to assist drainage.

Turfing a lawn is only feasible where good quality turf can be obtained at a reasonable price. Rough, coarse grassed turf costs just as much money to lay, but no amount of time or money will turn it into a respectable lawn. The advantage of turf over seed is that it provides an instant lawn.

Turf can be laid at any time when weather and soil con-ditions permit, avoiding only periods of severe drought or frost. Levelling the site is the same whether turfing or seed-ing. By working from a pre-determined level, path, house wall or drive, by means of pegs and a plank, the merest begin-ner, with the help of a spirit level, can make absolutely sure of a professionally finished sur-face. This makes seed sowing or laying turf simple.

The soil should be firmed but not over compacted, then lightly raked to leave the surface loose so the grass roots penetrate quickly into it. This applies whether turfing or seeding.

Ten days prior to grassing down apply a light fertilizer dressing of nitrogen, phosphates, and potash. The John Innes

Base fertilizer or one of the many proprietary products will do very well.

Turfing

Make sure the turf is of good quality, with finer leaved grasses predominating and reasonably free from weeds. Usually turfs are supplied in lengths of 36 inches by 12 inches by $1\frac{1}{2}$ inches deep ($90 \times 30 \times 4$ cm).

Lay the turf in straight rows across the plot. Alternate rows are staggered so the joints between the rows do not follow through, exactly as the joints in a well built wall are broken. This enables the turves to knit together quickly into a unified whole (*see centre right*).

A mixture of sand or compost and grass seed brushed into the crevices will help with the bonding.

Seeding

Preparation of the soil is similar for turfing and may be carried out at any time during the growing season when the soil is moist enough. Late Spring or early Autumn are the most suitable periods.

Choose a grass seed according to the type of lawn required. The fine-leaved grasses take longer to germinate, need careful mowing and feeding but are the most attractive to look at.

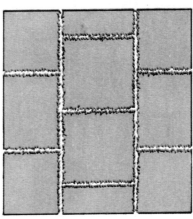

Above. A weed-free, well tended lawn provides the ideal backcloth to the flamboyant colours of bedding roses.

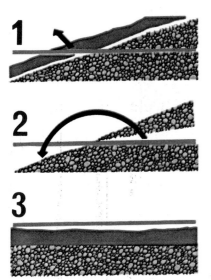

The coarser mixtures, including rye grass, are hard wearing and easier to maintain but never look quite so good as the fine-leaved fescues and bents. Fine-leaved mixtures are expensive, the price grading down as the proportion of coarser grasses increases.

Mark the area to be sown with canes or a garden line into squares one metre by one metre. Two ounces (60 g) of grass seed will be enough to sow each square. Rake the seed lightly in. Under good conditions germination will take place within four days. Water should be applied if the weather turns dry.

When the grass is $2\frac{1}{2}$–3 inches (6–7 cm) high (seed or turf) it must be cut with a sharp blade mower, with the height adjusted so as just to tip the grass. Cutting thereafter is done at twice weekly intervals, gradually lowering the blades to the normal level.

Lawn Care

No lawn newly made or established should ever be close shaved or bare patches will certainly occur to encourage moss and weeds.

Lawns need feeding at regular intervals during the growing season. This begins in mid Spring during warm moist weather. The fertilizer used should contain a high proportion of nitrogen to stimulate leaf growth. The grass box may be removed so the clippings are returned to the lawn during periods of dry weather to act as a moisture conserving mulch. Where possible feeding should continue at intervals of six weeks. Apply the last feed in late Summer reducing the nitrogen, and increasing the potash so growth is hardened down for the Winter.

Never mow the lawn when it is very wet; it compacts the soil too much.

Never leave the grass box off in wet weather, it encourages fungal disease.

Never neglect feeding.

Avoid high phosphatic fertilizers; they tend to encourage clover and the coarser grasses.

Where weeds are a problem regular applications of selective weed killer, either incorporated with the fertilizer or used separately, will eliminate the nuisance. By feeding the lawn three or four days before applying the weed killer, growth is stimulated and, as the weeds die, the grass spreads in to fill the empty space.

Routine cultivations include *spiking*, particularly during the Autumn, with a hollow tined fork. This takes out a cone of soil, relieves surface compaction, allowing air and water to penetrate stimulating healthy root growth.

Raking or scarifying the turf with a wire rake removes the dead mat of grass which accumulates at soil level.

Top dressings may be applied after the spiking and raking. Brushed into the surface they help keep the holes left by the spiking open, and improve the physical condition of the soil.

Winter Maintenance

Worn or diseased patches in the lawn may be repaired as opportunity offers.

Bare patches: Remove the soil from the offending area. Cut a patch of turf slightly larger than the hole it is to fill, so when fitted into place the centre stands higher than the surrounding level. In a short while it will settle to leave no visible sign of the repair.

Diseased patches should be removed, treated with a fungicide and similarly repaired.

Lawn edges frequently get broken down by frost or careless feet. The damaged portion may be cut out as shown (**1**). Turn the turf round so a clean unbroken edge is faced onto the border or path, and the damaged edge is to the lawn (**2**). The broken portion is levelled up with compost, then in Spring is sown with a good quality

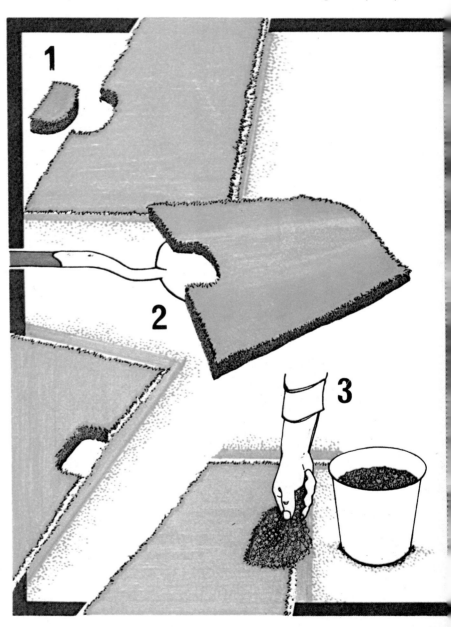

lawn seed mixture (3).

Moss in the lawn is a sure indication of the gardener's neglect. At the first sign of infestation try to discover the cause. It could be surface compaction which spiking alleviates; starvation which the feeding programme outlined previously will correct; poor drainage which once the lawn is laid takes some correcting. Scalping the lawn by over-close mowing leaves bare patches open to colonization by moss and weeds.

Special moss killers may be used but will only prove a temporary measure, because they only treat the symptoms instead of curing the illness.

Lawn sand used at intervals during the growing season kills weeds or moss and feeds the lawn at the same time. Lawn sand is made by mixing:

1 part (by weight) of calcined sulphate of iron.

3 parts (by weight) sulphate of ammonia.

20 parts (by weight) lime-free sand, which in addition to acting as a carrier to the chemical helps improve surface drainage.

Spread the material evenly over the lawn. The grass promptly turns black but quickly recovers while moss and weeds are killed.

Selective weed killers do not harm the grass, but make certain no spray drifts on to borders or vegetable plots, or a great deal of damage may be done.

Specific weed destroyers are made for the more persistent weeds like clover and speedwell. Always keep a watering can or knapsack sprayer for the use of selective weed killers only. By regular cutting and balanced feeding, weeds rarely become a problem.

Fungus diseases, fusarium patch is an example, frequently appear in late Summer. This should be treated with one of the proprietory fungicides available.

Always keep the mower blades sharp, the machine well maintained. Cut little and often.

Never scalp the grass.

Feed, spike and *rake* at regular intervals.

Do not roll a lawn. Do not lime a lawn except on professional advice as it encourages coarse grass.

Once a routine is established based on the above principles the lawn develops few problems.

Trees and Shrubs

Trees and shrubs show such a wide variety in shape, size, foliage and flower colour it would be reasonable to assume that one at least can be found to suit every garden. They play such a dominant and permanent part in the landscape that as much care should be taken in their selection as is lavished on choosing the decor for the living room.

Both trees and shrubs divide readily into two broad groups. Those which retain their leaves throughout the year, collectively referred to as evergreens, include holly, yew and Scots pine; plants which contribute so much to the natural beauty of the landscape. In contrast, deciduous plants shed their leaves for a period then grow a completely new set.

Fastigiate

Open

Symmetrical

Rounded

Weeping

Standard

Bush

Half Standard

37

Acid and Alkaline Shrubs

Only the gardener-owner can decide what tree or shrub will prove most suitable in a given situation, but before planting anything check whether the soil is acid or alkaline. Some of the most beautiful shrubs will not grow in a lime soil. These include Rhododendron, Camellia, Calluna, Kalmia, Pernettya, Gaultheria, and Lithospermum.

Shrubs are expensive, so rather than trying to persuade a lime-hating plant to accept a lime soil, money would be better spent on a lime-tolerant plant in the first place. There is a long enough list to choose from: Potentilla, Buddleia, Cytisus, Berberis, Philadelphus, Daphne, Chaenomeles, Genista, Cotoneaster, Forsythia, and Ribes are just a few.

People gardening on an acid soil have an advantage in that the plants which normally grow in lime soil are quite capable of adapting and growing equally well on an acid soil. Forsythia looks just as well for example on an acid clay as it does in the free draining lime, but rhododendrons or heathers will under no circumstances tolerate the reverse conditions. They will only grow on an acid soil.

Pernettya mucronata

Acer palmatum 'Atropurpureum'

Camellia 'Donation'

Calluna vulgaris 'Alba'

Lithospermum 'Heavenly Blue'

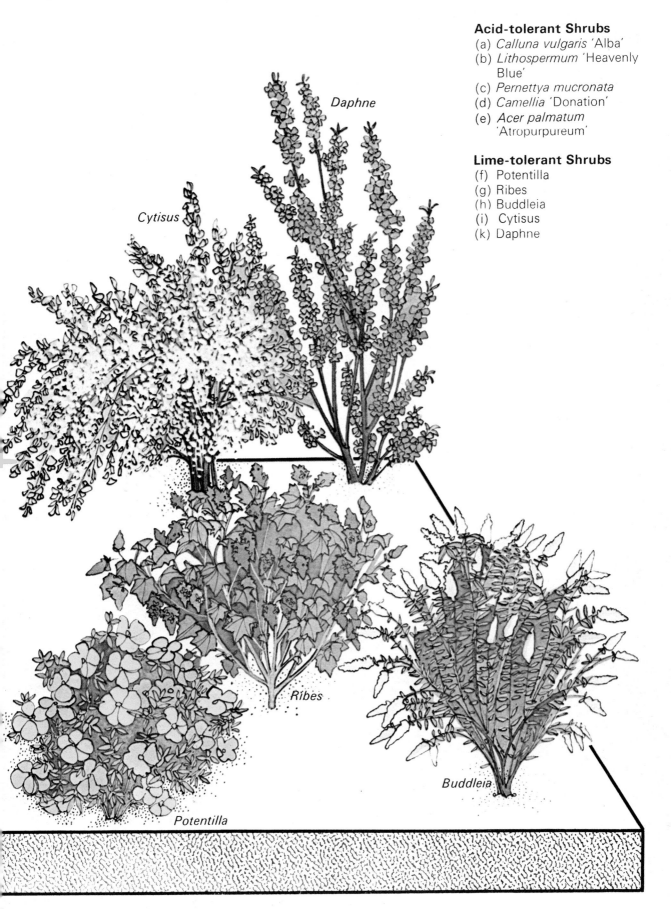

Acid-tolerant Shrubs
(a) *Calluna vulgaris* 'Alba'
(b) *Lithospermum* 'Heavenly Blue'
(c) *Pernettya mucronata*
(d) *Camellia* 'Donation'
(e) *Acer palmatum* 'Atropurpureum'

Lime-tolerant Shrubs
(f) Potentilla
(g) Ribes
(h) Buddleia
(i) Cytisus
(k) Daphne

Daphne

Cytisus

Ribes

Buddleia

Potentilla

Important Points

No shrub should be planted until the soil has been thoroughly prepared because once established the shrub border is impossible to renovate, unlike the herbaceous border which can be lifted completely.

Double digging, as described in the chapter on soils, improves the physical condition of the soil by working in plenty of organic matter. The old saying 'look after the roots and the top looks after itself' is nowhere better applied than to shrub gardening.

Leave the soil rough over Winter to weather, check to see if lime is required, then in late Winter work in a complete fertilizer dressing at 4 oz per square yard (100 g/m²). This ensures that nutrient is readily available when the roots take hold.

Do not immediately rush out and buy the first 2 dozen shrubs which take your fancy. Look at the garden, then shrubs and trees can be bought to suit a particular position, not the reverse. Note the position of drains and house foundations as tree roots can do enormous damage to both.

Planting for *deciduous* shrubs can be carried out whenever the weather is suitable during the dormant period. *Evergreens* will respond to planting either just as growth slows down for the dormant period or just as it recommences in Spring.

Containerisation. The practice of growing plants in pots or containers enables both deciduous and evergreen shrubs or trees to be planted all the year round.

Do not plant when the soil is bog wet.

Do not plant when conditions are very dry.

Humid conditions are the best, they stop leaves losing moisture which damaged roots cannot replace. Damaged or dead roots should be cut back to sound wood. Dig a hole large enough to accommodate the roots spread out to their fullest extent. If a stake is necessary mark the place with a cane before back filling the soil. Staking should be done on the

Wind shelter is particularly important for newly planted evergreens. This can either be of polythene or hessian, open on the side away from the prevailing winds to give a degree of air circulation so that the plant is not encouraged in early growth when it is easily damaged by a late spring frost.

Although not included in the select list *Laburnum × 'vossii'* has such a magnificent presence that, used as a dominant part of a shrub border, it makes a focal point in the garden. Colour plants round it should be such as to complement rather than contrast with the long yellow racemes of the Laburnum. In the illustration the associate planting includes the ground cover Hosta which will produce flowers later in the season and the complementary flowers of the "lilac" which always seem to give the right colour balance with the Laburnum yellow. Care should be taken in planting this tree if you have small children because the seeds are poisonous.

windward side so the tree blows away from and not onto the support. Work the soil carefully back amongst the roots, if necessary by hand, firming as the work proceeds, but leaving the surface loose so air and moisture have ready access. The finished level should come just above the stain on the stem which indicates the depth to which the tree was planted in the nursery. Drive a stake in to replace the cane, and secure the tree to it with one of the many patent ties available which, while giving support, allows the tree

frost damage.

Keep the weeds down either with a hoe, or paraquat weed killer which kills without harming soil or plants provided it touches no green leaves. The chemical acts only through the chlorophyll so can be sprayed onto brown stems without fear of damage. Indeed, it can be used to kill suckers from grafted plants like cherries and roses. Otherwise they must be pulled out by hand, first removing the soil so the offending root can be traced back to the stem then pulled clean away.

Hedges are without doubt the cheapest and most effective way of placing a barrier between gardens as a wind shield or to give privacy. Shrubs used for hedges must have the following qualifications: they must be cheap, adaptable to soil and climate, and easy to maintain with attractive flowers or foliage. Many can be raised *from seed* at the expenditure of a little time and effort, for example: beech, holly, quickthorn, and cotoneaster.

Cuttings: Forsythia, Ribes, and roses are just a few which root easily.

In most cases the gardener will not wish to wait two or three years for results and will buy from a reputable nurseryman. This cannot be over-emphasised: buy from a reputable source. Nurserymen are only too pleased to help with advice in most cases.

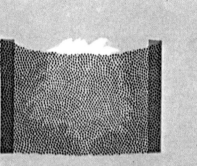

to grow without interference. String ties, unless regularly checked can cut into bark as the stem grows until the tree strangles to death (*see right*).

Regular watering, especially over the foliage in dry weather, cuts down transpiration loss and creates the sort of humid atmosphere which promotes rapid growth.

There is a transplanting liquid which, sprayed over the foliage of newly transplanted trees and shrubs, seals them in a film of plastic which lasts long enough for the roots to have penetrated into the soil once more. Well worth using for valuable or difficult shrubs or trees.

A mulch of peat, compost or rotted manure each year in late Spring will keep up the soil condition, plus regular feeding, but not so as to force soft growth which is prone to disease and

Select List 1

Popular hedging plants of proven reliability are comparatively few in number, but almost any shrub which will stand hard pruning can be used.

Prepare the site as for border planting.

A choice can be made from the following.

*means average ** means good *** means very good.*

Evergreen Hedges

* Berberis darwinii Ht 6–8 ft (1·8–2·4 m). Orange. Flowers in Spring, followed by purple berries. Plant 2 ft (60 cm) apart. Trim as flowers fade or in mid-Summer.

** Berberis x stenophylla Ht 8–10 ft (2·4–3·0 m). Yellow scented flowers, in Spring. Plant 30 inches (75 cm) apart. Trim as flowers fade.

Both may be propagated by

Buxus

Crataegus

Chamaecyparis lawsoniana

means of cuttings, or in the case of stenophylla by suckers.

Buxus sempervirens "Common Box", in its various forms offers good hedging plants. Plant at 18 inches (45 cm) apart. Trim as required in Summer. Propagate by cuttings in late Summer. Suitable varieties:

** *B.s.* 'Handsworthensis'.

** *B.s.* 'Latifolia maculata', blotched yellow leaves.

*** × *Cupressocyparis leylandii* makes a very effective tall hedge, a most desirable conifer in every respect. Plant at 30 inches (75 cm) apart. Trim in late Spring or early Autumn. Under good conditions this conifer will grow 30 inches (75 cm) a year.

*** *Chamaecyparis lawsoniana* 'Green Hedge' also earns the top award, though much slower growing. A hedge I cultivated for 14 years reached 10 ft (3·0 m) in height without needing trimming. Plant at 30 inches (75 cm).

Propagate × *Cupressocyparis leylandii* and 'Green Hedge' by cuttings.

** *Ligustrum* "Privet". A plant tolerant of soil and climatic conditions to a remarkable degree. All propagate readily from cuttings.

** *L. japonicum* "Japanese Privet". Plant at 1 ft (30 cm) apart. Ht 6 ft (1·8 m).

* *L. ovalifolium* in all its forms is much used as a hedging plant. Planted 5 of the type to 3 of the yellow leaved 'Aureum', it makes a colourful boundary to the garden. Ht 6 ft (1·8 m).

* *Lonicera nitida* plant at 18 inches (45 cm). Needs clipping frequently. Ht 6 ft (1·8 m).

*** *Taxus baccata* is a top class hedging plant, making a close, near impenetrable barrier up to 20 ft (6·1 m) high, but it grows rather slowly. Plant at 18 inches (45 cm) apart. Trim in late Summer.

Deciduous Hedges

* *Crataegus monogyna* "Hawthorn" is a good hedge for gardens bordering on farm land. Seed stratified then sown will provide material for making a hedge in three years. Plant at 15 inches (38 cm) apart. Trim as required.

*** *Fagus sylvatica* "Common Beech", again can be raised from seed. Space at 12—18 inches (30—45 cm) apart. Do not clip for the first 3—4 years, thereafter in late Summer. Ht 10—20 ft (3·0—6·1 m). An added attraction is that the dry bronze foliage is retained throughout the Winter.

** *Prunus cerasifera* 'Pissardii' makes a most attractive tapestry hedge if planted in the ratio 3 to 2 with the green leaved type plant, *P. cerasifera* 'Myrobaln B'. Space the bushes 20 inches (50 cm) apart, and trim as required, usually twice a year.

Some of the modern shrub roses make first class hedges:

'Fred Loads', orange red.

'Grace Abounding'. creamy apricot.

'Queen Elizabeth', pink.

'Heidelburg', dark red.

Any shrub mentioned in the detailed list of trees and shrubs if suitable as a hedge has been starred accordingly.

Prunus
cerasifera

Ligustrum

Taxus

Fagus

Select List 2

Robinia pseudoacacia

Before making a selection find out the size and ultimate spread of each individual tree and shrub. Shape is important. In a small garden a fastigiate tree would be suitable, whereas on an open plan housing estate there would be room for one of pendulous habit.

Six Flowering or Fruiting Trees Suitable for the Small Garden

Cotoneaster — salicifolia flocossus' up to 15 ft (4·6 m) high by 8 ft (2·4 m) across. White flowers in late Spring, followed by masses of scarlet berries in Autumn.

Malus 'Profusion' a beautiful crab apple, flowers wine red, fragrant, young leaves copper. Ht 15 ft (4·6 m). Spread 10 ft (3·0 m).

Prunus 'Amanogawa' very upright in growth, fragrant pink flowers, semi-double in Spring. Ht 15 ft (4·6 m). Spread 6 ft (1·8 m).

P. sargentii, a rather taller tree, up to 30 ft (9·1 m), making a round headed tree, pink flowers in late Spring and glorious autumn colour.

Pyrus salicifolia "Willow Leaved Pear", a graceful weeping tree up to 15 ft (4·6 m) high with cream flowers in late Spring. Possibly because of the attractive foliage should have been in the next section.

Sorbus hybrida 'Fastigiata' up to 20 ft (6·1 m) high by 8 ft (2·4 m) spread. Leaves grey green, fruit in large clusters — scarlet.

All the trees listed will tolerate most soils, acid or alkaline. All need the minimum amount of pruning to keep them in good condition.

Six Trees with Beautiful Foliage or Stems

Acer griseum "Paper Barked Maple". Ht 20 ft (6·1 m) × 8 ft (2·4 m). Cinnamon coloured bark. Scarlet autumn colour.

Betula pendula 'Youngii', mushroom headed weeping tree 12—15 ft (3·6—4·6 m) high. Silver bark and delicate foliage.

Ilex aquifolium 'Flavescens', 15 ft (4·6 m). Leaves suffused yellow, making this a good specimen plant against a dark background.

Malus tschonoskii, up to 23 ft (7·0 m) high by 10 ft (3 m) across. The Autumn colour is a superb blend of orange, scarlet and purple.

Robinia pseudoacacia 'Frisia', delightful small round headed tree 20 ft (6·1 m) by 12 ft (3·6 m) across. Leaves rich golden yellow from late Spring until Autumn.

Sorbus aria 'Lutescens', up to 25 ft (7·6 m) high. Leaves a creamy white in Spring, becoming glaucous grey.

Six Conifers for the Small Garden

Chamaecyparis lawsoniana 'Columnaris', very upright with glaucous grey foliage, 20 ft (6·1 m) high.

C. lawsoniana 'Stewartii', a little tall possibly at 35 ft (10·7 m) for the small garden, but one of the best golden conifers over a wide range of soils.

Juniperus chinensis 'Columnaris Glauca', very upright dense foliaged tree up to 20 ft (6·1 m) high with grey green foliage.

J. communis "Irish Juniper", up to 14 ft (4·3 m) high, the silver grey foliage and very

Prunus 'Amanogawa'

erect growth make this a good proposition for the small garden. *Picea pungens* 'Koster', this popular silver blue spruce makes a small tree 25 ft (7·6 m) high, but it is so slow growing. Makes a worthy addition to the small garden.

Taxus baccata 'Fastigiata Aureo-marginata', an upright golden form of the Irish yew which makes an attractive specimen small tree where space is at a premium.

Climbing and Wall Plants

The space offered by a wall or fence adds another dimension to the garden landscape. The shelter afforded means that shrubs liable to frost damage in the open garden survive unscathed.

The soil immediately against the wall or fence is often dust dry and devoid of food, so replace this with a mixture of loam and well rotted compost or manure. The supports should be nailed to wooden bobbins so they stand off from the wall permitting the air to circulate freely, reducing the risk of disease.

Clematis, amongst the loveliest of climbing plants, are also versatile. They can be grown on a wall, over outbuildings, fences, tree stumps, or any shrub which will tolerate the competition. Clematis prefer a light, cool, moist soil, well drained and alkaline. 'Shade at the roots, head in the sun' is a good maxim to follow when growing clematis. A selection as follows:

Clematis macropetala 'Markham's Pink', deep pink flowers. Summer months.

Clematis montana rubens, bronze young growths, pink flowers. Summer months.

Clematis viticella 'Royal Velours', velvet purple flowers in late Summer.

Large flowered hybrids include the following:

'Comtesse de Bouchaud', soft rose pink. Mid-late Summer.

'Ernest Markham', deep glowing red. Mid Summer—early Autumn.

'Jackmanii Superba', rich violet purple. Mid Summer — early Autumn.

'Nelly Moser', pale pink with a carmine central bar. Early Summer, repeat late Summer.

The montana section may be left unpruned except for removal of dead and overcrowded branches.

Late Summer flowering varieties e.g. 'Jackmanii Superba' may, if thought necessary, be cut back to within two or three buds of the old wood in late Winter — left unpruned the stems become bare at the base.

Eccremocarpus scaber is useful as a climber for quick coverage because it can be grown from seed to flower in a single season. The orange scarlet flowers are borne profusely throughout the Summer.

Hedera helix "Ivy" has no equal amongst self-clinging climbing plants. Ivies will thrive under the poorest soil conditions and will put up with a considerable degree of atmospheric pollution or shade.

H. helix 'Buttercup', rich golden yellow leaves.

H. helix 'Congesta', a slow growing plant with three-lobed leaves.

H. helix 'Cavendishii', with mottled grey leaves.

Hydrangea petiolaris, self clinging climber. White flowers in mid Summer.

Jasminum nudiflorum is a gem producing flowers of deep yellow in the depth of Winter, even when planted on a north wall.

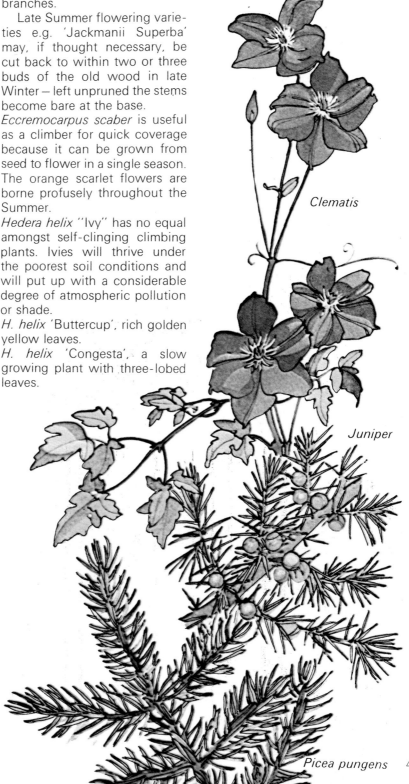

Clematis

Juniper

Picea pungens   45

Select List 3

Jasminum officinale 'Common White Jasmine'. With the most delightfully fragrant flowers in late Summer.

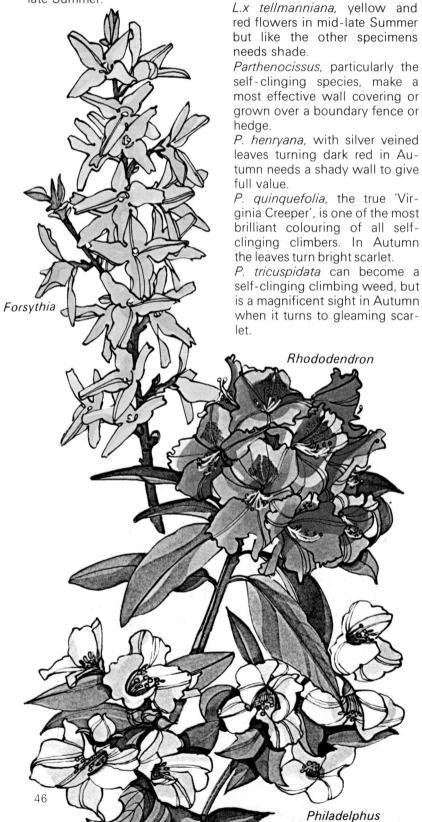

Forsythia

Rhododendron

Philadelphus

Lonicera periclymenum 'Woodbine' evokes memories of cottage gardens and fragrant country lanes. Flowers creamy white flushed pink. Summer months. A cool leafy soil and partial shade are advisable.

L.x tellmanniana, yellow and red flowers in mid-late Summer but like the other specimens needs shade.

Parthenocissus, particularly the self-clinging species, make a most effective wall covering or grown over a boundary fence or hedge.

P. henryana, with silver veined leaves turning dark red in Autumn needs a shady wall to give full value.

P. quinquefolia, the true 'Virginia Creeper', is one of the most brilliant colouring of all self-clinging climbers. In Autumn the leaves turn bright scarlet.

P. tricuspidata can become a self-clinging climbing weed, but is a magnificent sight in Autumn when it turns to gleaming scarlet.

Schizophragma hydrangioides supports itself like the ivy by aerial roots. Small creamy white flowers are borne in flattened heads during mid Summer.

Wisteria floribunda in all its forms is a delightful bush. The lilac purple flowers have a unique fragrance.

W. sinensis is equally splendid when the racemes of deep lilac flowers exude their fragrance on a warm mid Summer evening.

Six Shrubs which Flower in Spring

Daphne mezereum flowers in early Spring, the purple red petals have a fragrance which is most pleasant. The flowers are carried on growth made the previous Summer, and wreath the leafless branches. Ht 3 ft (90 cm). Propagate from seed.

Magnolia stellata, white petalled flowers in Spring. Ht 5 ft (1·5 m). Propagate semi-hardwood cuttings.

Forsythia 'Lynwood' flowers rich yellow profusely over the whole bush in Spring. Prune out old worn out wood to shape the bush every three years. Propagate semi-hardwood cuttings.

Berberis × lologensis, a beautiful evergreen shrub. 6 ft (1·8 m) high in maturity smothered each year during late Spring with apricot coloured flowers.

Rhododendron 'Elizabeth', scarlet, 3 ft (90 cm), 'Pink Pearl' 8 ft (2·4 m), 'Susan' mauve 4 ft (1·2 m) (if the soil is acid). Propagated by layers.

Syringa "Lilac", 'Hugo Koster', purple crimson, 'Marechal Foch', carmine rose (if the soil is lime); 'Vestale', white.

Cytisus × praecox, deep cream flowers mounded over a 3 ft (90 cm) high bush in late Spring.

Summer Flowering Shrubs

Escallonia 'Donard Radiance', evergreen shrub. 4 ft (1·2 m). Flowers intense rose red. Propagate by semi-hardwood cuttings. Prune after flowering; can be used as a hedge.

Potentilla fruticosa 'Day Dawn', pink flowers carried on a 3 ft (90 cm) high bush throughout the Summer.

Genista hispanica, rounded bush up to 3 ft (90 cm) high. Masses of yellow flowers in mid Summer. Likes a hot dry position.

Calluna vulgaris 'Peter Sparkes', demands an acid soil where it grows 30 inches (75 cm) high, long spikes of deep pink double flowers appear in late Summer. Cuttings taken when flowering finished.

Hypericum patulum 'Hidcote' (on a lime soil), semi-evergreen, deep yellow saucer-shaped flowers. Summer—early Autumn. Ht 4 ft (1·2 m). Propagate by cuttings in Autumn or by division in Spring.

Philadelphus 'Belle Etoile', shrub up to 5 ft (1·5 m) high, fragrant white flowers flushed maroon. Mid Summer. Cuttings in late Summer.

Hebe armstrongii, golden foliage, white flowers in late Summer.

Shrubs for Autumn

Hydrangea (various). Ht 4–8 ft (1·2–2·4 m). Flowers blue to dark red. Late Autumn. Cuttings early Autumn.

Fuchsia 'Mrs Popple'. Ht 3 ft (90 cm). Flowers red and purple. Autumn months. Cuttings early Autumn.

Romneya coulteri. Ht 6 ft (1·8 m). Flowers white with central boss of yellow stamens. Autumn. Propagate by root cuttings in late Autumn.

Berberis 'Barbarossa'. Ht 6 ft. Red berries in clustered masses in Autumn.

Acer palmatum 'Atropurpureum'. Autumn colour of leaves a rich glowing red. Grafted on to seedling Acer palmatum.

Viburnum davidii grow both male and female evergreen shrubs 3 ft (90 cm) high, turquoise blue fruits.

Winter Flowering Shrubs

Erica herbacea (E. carnea). 'Myretoun Ruby', up to 10 inches (25 cm) in height, dark green foliage, bright red flowers. Mid Winter to mid Spring. Cuttings in early Summer.

Hamamelis mollis 'Pallida'. Autumn leaf colour pale yellow, flowers carried on the leafless branches mid-late Winter. Sulphur yellow, delicately fragrant. Propagate by layers in Spring or grafting.

Mahonia japonica, the best of evergreen winter flowering shrubs. Ht 6–8 ft (1·8–2·4 m). Yellow, 'Lily of the Valley' scented, racemes of flowers in late Winter. Propagation by seed stratified.

Viburnum × bodnantense, the best of deciduous winter blossoming shrubs. The pink and white scented flowers grace the branches from Autumn to mid Spring, whenever the weather is mild. Propagation: suckers or cuttings in early Autumn.

Prunus subhirtella 'Autumnalis', flowers white semi-double all over the 15 ft (4·6 m) high bush at intervals during the Winter.

Cornus mas 'Variegata', white margined leaves in Summer, yellow flowers in late Winter. Cuttings of semi-ripe wood root readily.

I have mentioned no cotoneaster, but *C. horizonatalis* and 'Hybridus Pendulus' are striking shrubs when covered with dark red berries.

Hamamelis

Syringa

Romneya

Herbaceous Perennials

A herbaceous perennial is a plant which at some period of the year, usually the Winter, loses all its leaves and stems back to soil level. Each Spring the top growth is renewed, so the above ground portions are annual, the roots perennial.

Because the tops do die back completely during part of the year, herbaceous borders provide only seasonal interest. For this reason they are frequently grown in association with shrubs which are capable of carrying interest through the Winter.

Before planting, the bed must be thoroughly prepared, preferably in the Autumn, which gives time for the soil to settle. Double digging, working plenty of organic matter into the trench bottom, as described on page 10, will do much to improve even the poorest soil. Leave the surface rough, the frost will break up the hard clods by the Spring. If lime is needed, a pH test will decide (see page 9).

Two weeks before planting in the Spring, when the soil is dry to walk on, fork in a dressing of complete fertilizer (nitrogen, phosphate and potash). A rough levelling down can be done at the same time.

Design is very important. Make the various groups irregular in shape. Bring a block of taller growing plants through almost to the front of the border so that interest is given to the design. Contrive the various groups so each individual member receives a fair share of light and air, ensuring healthy growth.

Perennials and Shrubs
Reading from left to right
Top row
Viburnum 'Dawn' (*Shrub*)
Delphinium 'Blue Haze'
Chamaecyparis lawsoniana
  'Fletcheri' (*Shrub*)
Lupinus 'Daydream'
Acer palmatum 'Atropurpureum'
  (*Shrub*)

Middle row
Anaphalis yedoensis
Rose 'Ballerina' (*Shrub*)
Hosta fortunei 'Albopicta'

Bottom row
Sedum 'Autumn Joy'
Veronica 'Crater Lake'
Doronicum 'Spring Beauty'

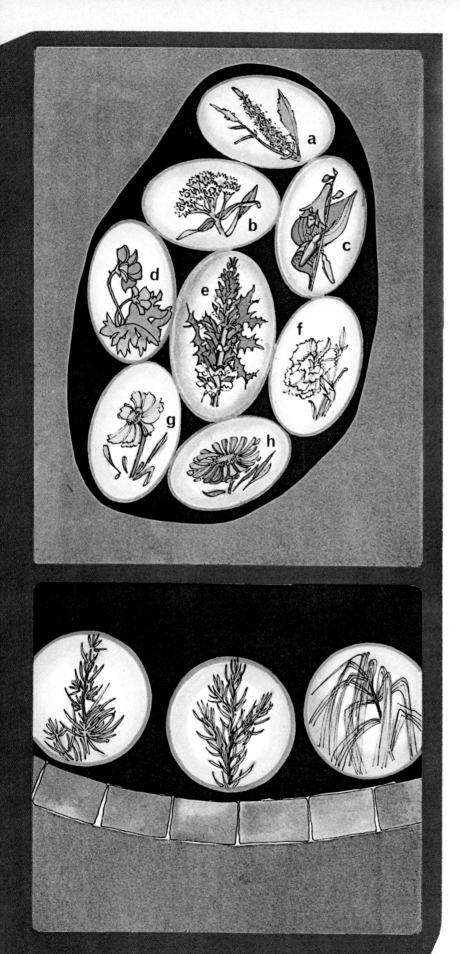

Featuring Herbaceous Perennials

An island bed in the centre of a lawn (*above left*) may be viewed from all sides. The taller plants in this case are kept towards the centre of the bed, grading down in height to the edge.

Plants do tend to encroach on the lawn. To make maintenance easier, edge the border with a line of flags or bricks (*below left*). They are hidden in Summer by foliage, and make a dry standing area during Winter work.

Some herbaceous perennials, hostas are a good example, are grown primarily for their attractive foliage. They can be used in bold groups (*above right*) to hide early flowering plants, which, if in full view, would make the border look untidy later in the year.

Ribbon borders lining a drive or house front may be planted with perennials instead of bedded out twice a year with annuals (see page 74). The plants selected must be low growing with good foliage or a long flowering season.

Corner Site with Hostas

a *Berberis darwinii*
b Delphinium 'Peter Pan'
c Lupin 'Lady Fayre'
d *Anaphalis yedoensis*
e Rose 'Nevada'
f Kniphofia 'Brimstone'
g *Paeonia mlokosewitschii*
h *Aster thomsonii* 'Nanus'
i *Campanula latiloba* 'Percy Piper
j Doronicum 'Spring Beauty'
k *Hosta fortunii* 'Aureomarginata'
l *Anaphalis yedoensis*
m Tradescantia 'Isis'
n *Hosta undulata* 'Medio-variegata'

Obtaining the Best Results

Planting is carried out in the Spring as the soil begins to warm up. Firm the roots well so there are no air pockets left to inhibit that intimate contact between root and soil. Do not over-firm, particularly on a clay soil, or the unfortunate plants will be left standing in a pool of water after every shower of rain.

Staking may be necessary with some of the taller growing varieties. Put the supports in position early, for once the stems start to be blown about tying them in is laborious.

Canes, square stakes, wire hoops or even twiggy pieces pruned from the shrubs all make suitable supports. Whatever the material used it should be as inconspicuous as possible. Nothing looks worse than a perennial border which displays more stakes than flowers.

Twice each year during the life of the border feed with a complete fertilizer: 3 oz per square yard (105 g/m²) in early Spring, and 2 oz per square yard (70 g/m²) in early Summer.

Herbaceous plants make a lot of growth each year, and to do this successfully the fertility of the bed has to be maintained. After the first fertilizer application put a thin layer of compost, peat, or rotted manure on top of the soil to conserve moisture.

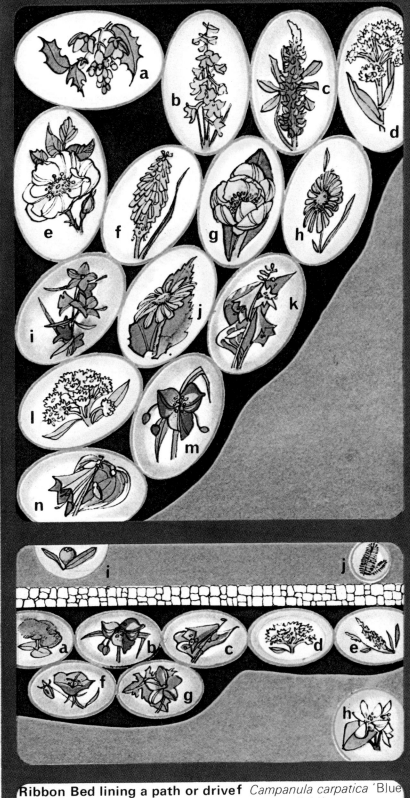

Ribbon Bed lining a path or drive

a Sedum 'Autumn Joy'
b Tradescantia 'Isis'
c *Hosta undulata* 'Medio-variegata'
d Anaphalis 'Summer Snow'
e Veronica 'Crater Lake'
f *Campanula carpatica* 'Blue Moonlight'
g *Geranium endressii* 'Wargrave Pink'
h Malus 'Wisley Crab'
i *Pyrus salicifolia*
j *Picea pungens* 'Glauca'

Select List 1

Acanthus longifolius Interesting foliage, spikes of long lasting mauve and white flowers on 30 inch (75 cm) stems. Can be used as a foil to the daisy-like flowers of Coreopsis. Succeeds in most soils.

Anaphalis yedoensis 'Pearly Everlasting', with silver leaves and everlasting white flower heads is a useful addition as a foliage contrast to reflect the brighter colours around. Best grown in a lighter soil, but will tolerate clay.

Aster × frikartii Tall growing with lavender daisy flowers on 3 ft (90 cm) stems. Divided and re-planted every two or three years it is very free flowering.

Aster novi-belgii The Michael-mas Daisy. 'Marie Ballard' blue 3 ft (90 cm) and 'Carnival' red 2 ft (60 cm) are just two varieties from the many on offer; cool moist soil suits them very well.

Aster thomsonii 'Nanus' A faultless, greyish foliage bush, starred with lavender blue flowers for months. Likes a position in full sun.

Astrantia maxima should be in every flower arranger's garden. The light rose flowers carried well above the foliage on 3 ft (90 cm) stems are most attractive. Most soils. Divide in Spring every 3 or 4 years.

Campanula The ever popular bell flowers offer such a wide selection of species that there should be something to suit every location from a window box to the grand demesne.

Campanula carpatica 'Blue-Moonlight' A neat mound of a plant 9 inches (23 cm) high covered in light blue flowers in mid Summer is a gem for the dwarf border. Cuttings in mid Spring.

Campanula glomerata 'Superba' Looks well with shrub roses, the violet flowers are held primly erect on 30 inch (75 cm) stems. Most soils. Sun or light shade.

Divide every 4–5 years.

Campanula latiloba 'Percy Piper' Slightly taller, yet only in the most exposed position will the 36 inch (90 cm) high stems clustered with deep blue flowers need staking.

Coreopsis verticillata 'Grandiflora' makes a neatly rounded bush which over many weeks is embellished with rich yellow flowers. 18 inches (45 cm) high. Most soils. Divide every 5–6 years.

Delphinium must rank amongst the best known of all herbaceous plants and enjoy a well deserved popularity. They can be propagated from seed, but for those

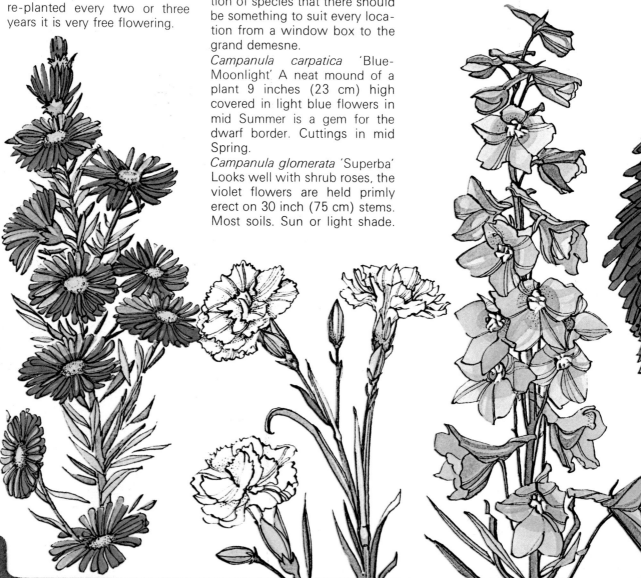

Aster novi-belgii 'Carnival'　　　　Dianthus 'Mrs Sinkins'　　　　Delphinium

who prefer the following are a selection of good named varieties:

'Blue Bees'. Pale blue, white eye. 4 ft (120 cm) high.

'C. F. Langdon' Lovely semi-double, clear mid blue. 6 ft (180 cm) high and almost the first to flower.

'Julia Langdon' Mauve semi-double flowers. A broad firm spike 5 ft (150 cm) high.

'F. W. Smith' Violet blue with a white eye. Semi-double. 4 ft (120 cm) high.

'Peter Pan' Mid blue flowers, is a good contrast to the last variety described 4 ft (120 cm) high.

Named varieties of delphinium are propagated from cuttings taken during early Spring, just as the plants start into growth. For those who like to gamble, seed sown in late Winter under glass will give flowering plants by late Summer, but these will not be true to the parent plant.

Dianthus For those who garden on a lime soil there are few border plants more attractive in both colour and fragrance.

Dianthus × allwoodii offers several varieties which are hardy with a good long flowering season. 'Doris' and 'London Poppet' one pink, the other laced red are value for money.

Border Pinks. 'Mrs Sinkins' double white and very fragrant, and 'Mrs Pilkington' double light pink make a delightful edge to a border.

All dianthus may be propagated from cuttings or pipings taken in early/mid Summer. A handful of sharp sand worked into the soil beside the parent plant provides suitable compost. Insert the cuttings then cover them with one upturned 2 lb (1 kg) jam jar.

Doronicum 'Spring Beauty' opens fully double yellow flowers in mid Spring so is well worth inclusion even in the select border. Height 15 inches (38 cm). A moist soil in full sun is ideal.

Eryngium variifolium succeeds best in a light sandy soil where the evergreen marbled leaves and silver blue flower spikes can develop their full character. For heavier soils *E. oliverianum* would be more reliable. Deeply divided flowers. Height 3 ft (90 cm).

Both varieties can be propagated by means of seed, root cuttings or careful division just as growth commences in Spring.

Euphorbia griffithii 'Fire Glow' is a plant which is not easy to restrict in limited space. Where room can be permitted for a colony the deep orange flower heads make a most impressive spectacle in early Summer. Height 24–30 inches (60–75 cm), and it is happy in most soils.

Kniphofia   Coreopsis   *Helleborus niger*   Hosta   53

Select List 2

Geranium, popularly known as cranesbill are very adaptable in regard to soil, but care is needed to select those varieties with the longest flowering season.

Geranium endressii 'A. T. Johnson' with pink flowers throughout the Summer and only 18 inches (45 cm) in height is noteworthy.

Geranium wallichianum 'Buxtons Variety' produces deep blue flowers from late Summer into Autumn. A little dwarfer but more spreading at 12 inches (30 cm). Cuttings or division offer a ready means of increase.

Helleborus though designated as shade lovers, flower more profusely in northern areas when grown in full sun. Of all the species Helleborus niger "Christmas Rose" is the best loved. The pure white flowers anticipating Spring, compete with the snowdrops for pride of place. A cool, leafy soil suits very well. Propagation by means of seed sown immediately it is ripe.

Helleborus orientalis, my own favourite, is more adaptable in regard to soil with flowers ranging in colour from white, through crimson to dark purple. Seed germinates so readily it forms an easy way of increasing stock. The height is fairly constant at 18 inches (45 cm).

Hosta "Plantain Lily" makes such an impressive contribution to the border with remarkable foliage that the groups included must be sited with some care. The height varies between the species from 12—36 inches (30—90 cm).

Hosta fortunei 'Albopicta'. At 24 inches (60 cm) high has yellow leaves edged with green. H. tardiflora a charming dwarf species is only 12 inches (30 cm) high with deep lilac flowers appearing in early Autumn. H. undulata 'Medio-variegata' at 18 inches (45 cm) is a little taller, the white and green striped leaves are corrugated.

Division of the plants is best carried out just as growth commences in Spring.

Kniphofia "Red Hot Poker" do not occupy the place in modern gardens which their beauty warrants. The first Winter after planting the crowns should be covered in frosty weather with straw, peat, or dry leaves.

Kniphofia 'Brimstone' lemon yellow 3 ft (90 cm) flowers, late Summer.

K. × erecta interesting and unusual because the flower tubes are carried upright instead of hanging down $3\frac{1}{2}$ ft (105 cm).

K. uvaria most commonly grown of all, orange scarlet

Geranium wallichianum   Doronicum   Lupin 'Fireglow'

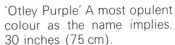

flowers on 4 ft (120 cm) stems in mid Summer.

A light soil well supplied with moisture suits all their needs. Seed or division in early Spring offers two methods of propagation.

Lupinus "Lupin" of cottage gardens in the shape of the Russell hybrids are enjoying a new popularity. A light sandy soil is ideal but on no account plant into a freshly manured bed. Seed is available and even a modest pinch will produce enough of a colour range to satisfy any but the most demanding gardener. Named varieties are on offer. 'Blue Jacket' deep blue, 'Fireglow' vivid orange, and 'Lady Fayre' soft rose can be relied on. Propagation of these is usually by means of cuttings taken in Spring rather than division.

Paeonia. Paeonies occupy a special place in the gardeners' affection and they enjoy the deeply worked soil of a well prepared herbaceous border. Beginning with the yellow flowered *P. mlokosewitschii* in late Spring, the season by a selection of varieties can be extended into mid Summer.

'Globe of Light', deep rose pink.

'Felix Crousse', crimson.

'Sarah Bernhardt', pale pink.

The old *P. officinalis* 'Alba Plena' of cottage gardens is still a good white to add a contrast. Do not divide unless absolutely necessary and then only in early Spring.

Phlox can present problems if grown too long without propagating new stock, but division or root cuttings offer such a ready means of increase that the problems are by no means insurmountable.

Cool moist conditions at the root are provided by working a little moist peat into the soil before planting. Reliable varieties which rarely need staking are:

'Balmoral' rosy lavender. 30 inches (75 cm).

'Otley Purple' A most opulent colour as the name implies. 30 inches (75 cm).

'Sandringham' Cyclamen pink with a dark eye.

'Mia Ruys' is a low growing white with large flower trusses on 24 inch (60 cm) stems.

Polemonium foliosissimum is a remarkable jacobs ladder in that, at least in my experience, it does not seed all over the garden. The lavender blue flowers open for several weeks. Height varies a little according to soil but averages out at about 24 inches (60 cm).

Sedum "Stonecrops" are a large versatile family. *Sedum spectabile* 'Brilliant' is almost worth a place on foliage quality alone, but when in early Autumn the leaves are embellished with large magenta rose flowers the picture is complete.

An open sunny position is to be advised to get best results. Growth is neat and compact up to 15 inches (38 cm).

Tradescantia 'Isis' The best of all the spider worts with flowering carried on continuously over many weeks. Deep blue. Height 18 inches (45 cm).

Veronica 'Crater Lake' is a neat floriferous speedwell. The deep blue spikes of flowers produced on 12 inch (30 cm) stems have all the clarity of colour for which the family is justly famous.

Polemonium   Veronica   Phlox   *Sedum spectabile*

Rock Plants

Rock plants are not difficult to grow. All they require is a well drained soil which is moisture-retentive enough to prevent drought conditions in Summer.

Stones (limestone, sandstone, millstone grit) are refinements which enable the gardener to present the plants in a natural manner. They are by no means essential, in fact, in a badly constructed rock garden, stones become a time consuming nuisance rather than an asset.

A well designed rock garden built from weathered limestone, or moss encrusted sandstone blocks, can, however, become a focal point. By careful alignment of the stones aspects can be provided to suit a plant's particular needs. Shade pockets for Primula or Ramonda, sun baked crevices for *Sepervivum* or "Silver Saxifraga".

Whatever method of construction is decided upon choose the most open site the garden offers. Drip from overhanging trees, root competition which robs the soil of moisture and nutriment, perpetual shade or draughts, limit the range of plants which can be grown to the scrubbiest of weeds. The most open position offers the light buoyant atmosphere mountain plants enjoy, and success is well nigh assured from the outset.

The first stage in construction is to make certain the ground is free from perennial weeds. Couch grass, docks, nettles and bind weed are impossible to eliminate once the stones are in position. If the chosen site is heavily weed-infested treat it with a total weed killer. Lesser problems can be dealt with by hand picking or rotovating.

Once the soil is clean it can be worked up into a condition to suit most of the more attractive rock plants' needs by a dressing of well rotted compost or moist peat and sharp sand. When the plants are in position a top dressing of quarter inch (6 mm) gravel or stone chippings will ensure the quick surface drainage so much a feature of the mountainous areas.

When a simulated mountain range effect is the aim, use

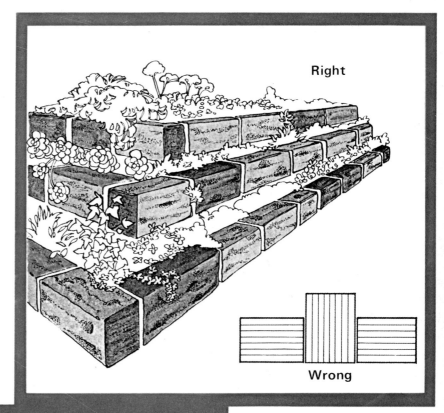

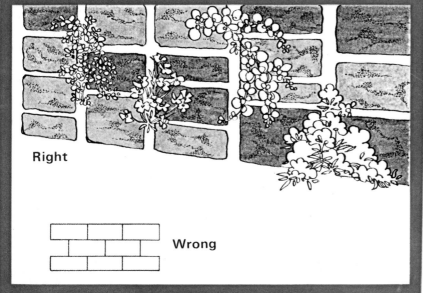

plain from one stone to another. Stones in a rock garden should be laid so the same principle applies with the rock grain running the same way throughout the whole structure (*see above*).

Ram the soil firm around each boulder so that no air spaces are left to form pools of stagnant moisture or hotels for mice. Each stone should 'butt' up to the next, but with a soil-packed crevice between for the plants.

Stones may be placed one on top of the other to gain extra height, but unlike the joints in a brick wall the crevices between the individual pieces should run right through the structure from top to bottom (*see left*).

limestone or sandstone blocks. Extra height can be gained and drainage improved by sinking the paths below the general level. A stream with a series of pools will also leave a surplus of soil to use as a basis for a miniature mountain.

Use the largest stones which can possibly be moved with the equipment available. Small stones stuck into a mound of soil

look more like an almond pudding than an alpine plateau and never give satisfaction. Bed the stones on their broadest surface, each block linked to the one alongside and tilted back to direct the moisture into the mound where the plant roots are.

Rocks have a grain, or strata as it is called. In nature the strata lines follow in the same

Alpine Table and Screes

For those gardeners who would like to grow rock plants without man-handling heavy blocks of stone, the alpine table or possibly a scree are a practical solution.

The alpine table (*see below*) as the name implies is a structure lifted anything from 6 to 40 inches (15–100 cm) above ground level. The best are those

pending on energy and enthusiasm, sloping at the bottom if the site is level to allow free drainage of surplus moisture.

Place 12–15 inches (30–38 cm) of broken stone in the bottom, covered with a thin layer of leaves or reversed turf on top to prevent the fine top mix of 5 parts gravel or stone chips, 3 parts soil, 2 parts peat and 1

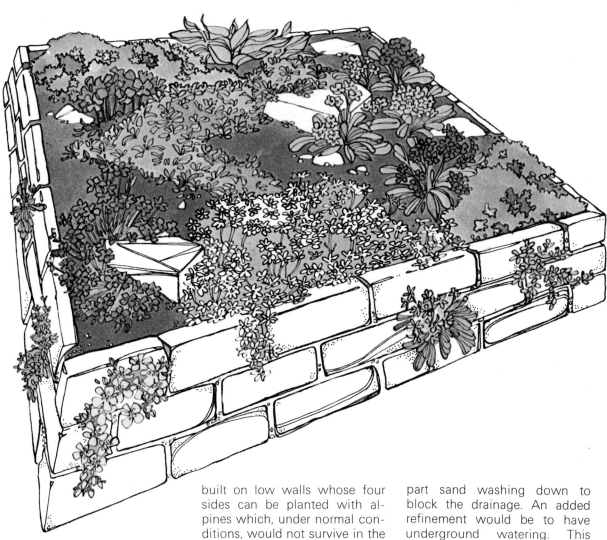

built on low walls whose four sides can be planted with alpines which, under normal conditions, would not survive in the open garden. The centre is filled with a mixture of 4 parts soil, 2 parts peat, 2 parts sand, and 2 parts $\frac{1}{4}$ inch (6 mm) stone chips or gravel. This is the type of free draining mixture alpines thrive in.

A scree (*top right*) is easiest to develop on a sloping site. The soil is excavated to a depth of 24–30 inches (60–75 cm), de-

part sand washing down to block the drainage. An added refinement would be to have underground watering. This simulates exactly conditions which apply in the mountains where seepage from melting snows keeps the roots constantly cool and moist.

Once the scree is planted up add a topping about 2 inches (5 cm) thick of gravel or stone chippings graded to $\frac{1}{4}$ inch (6 mm). In most gardens this is important to keep the neck of the plants dry in wet weather and act as a moisture retaining mulch in times of drought.

Screes are an easily managed method of cultivating Alpines and can be extremely colourful throughout the Spring and Summer months. Freely drained as they are, they suit the temperate needs of most Alpines to perfection: *Arenaria montana, Phlox douglasii* 'Rose Queen', *Euryops acraeus* and Veronica species.

Shrubs for the Rock Garden

Low growing shrubs are an integral part of a rock garden landscape. They give height to the planting in Summer and, in the case of dwarf conifers, prevent it being reduced to arid emptiness in Winter. Only those plants which are naturally dwarf should be included unless there is a lot of space to fill.

The golden foliaged form of the common juniper, *Juniperus communis* 'Depressa Aurea' is excellent ground cover even in full sun. Planted round with the blue *Viola albanica* and the yellow species *Tulipa tarda* it makes a beautiful picture in late Spring. The conifer grows about 10 inches (25 cm) high by 24 inches (60 cm) across.

Another slow growing conifer but upright in habit, the noah's ark pine, *Juniperus communis* 'Compressa', reaching a modest 10 inches (25 cm) after 20 years, makes a perfect vegetable cone.

Chamaecyparis obtusa 'Nana' makes a flat topped dome of soft golden foliage is a pleasant relief to the prevailing browns and fawns of Winter.

Flowering shrubs are invaluable if they are slow growing enough to maintain that exact feeling of proportion, so essential in a well designed rock garden.

Berberis × stenophylla 'Corallina Compacta' grows about 18 inches (45 cm) high by as much across. The flowers of this pleasant evergreen which appear in Spring are coral red in bud opening to bright yellow. With patience and persuasion cuttings taken with a heel in early Summer will grow.

Cotoneaster microphyllus thymifolius is a neat ground hugging shrub with shining deep green leaves. Cuttings are easy to root in early Summer.

Cytisus × beanii is possessed of the free flowering character of most brooms, but is prostrate enough to fit neatly into the rock garden. The golden yellow flowers appear in late Spring. A hot sun-baked position is ideal. Cuttings of half-ripened shoots available in early Summer will strike if inserted in sharp sand.

Euryops acraeus (*Evansii*) is a fairly recent introduction, but in a sunny well drained site makes a neat silver-leaved dome 12–15

dark green foliage — a shape to contrast with the general planting. After 20 years it stands 15–18 inches (38–45 cm) tall by 24 inches (50 cm).

Chamaecyparis lawsoniana 'Minima Aurea' is a dwarf conical very slow growing bush. The inches (30–38 cm) high. The yellow daisy flowers appear in early to mid Summer. Cuttings are taken in late Spring or late Summer.

Hebe 'Carl Teschner' makes a 12 inch (30 cm) bush of dark evergreen foliage. The small violet coloured flowers are carried in succession over many weeks. Cuttings root at almost any time in Summer.

Helianthemums, popularly known as rock roses, can be relied on to provide brilliant sheets of colour in any well drained soil baked by the sun. 'Firedragon' with orange scarlet

Chamaecyparis obtusa 'Nana'

Helianthemum 'Firedragon'

from late Spring until mid Autumn.

Rhododendron: the dwarf growing varieties are the most floriferous of evergreen rock garden shrubs, but do need an acid soil which is moisture-retentive.

'Blue Tit' is a neat blue flowered hybrid.

'Elizabeth' has bell shaped dark red flowers which appear in Spring, with a second crop in late Summer.

'Little Bert' is very compact, the waxy textured, deep red flowers nodding above dark green foliage.

Syringa velutina: a neat bushy lilac up to 30 inches (75 cm) high which opens lilac pink flowers possessed in full measure with the fragrance so characteristic of the better known tall varieties. Cuttings in early to mid Summer will strike.

flowers, 'Wisley Primrose' large yellow-cream flowers, or 'Cerise Queen' double red are reliable. All root readily from cuttings.

Iberis 'Little Gem' the compact, slow growing perennial candy tuft is a mound of white blossom in late Spring/early Summer and a neat foliaged plant for the rest of the season. Cuttings taken in mid Summer can usually be persuaded to root easily enough.

Lavandula nana 'Alba', a 12 inch (30 cm) tall, pale cream flowered lavender forms a pleasant contrast to the hot colours of the rock roses.

Lithospermum diffusum 'Heavenly Blue' needs a lime-free soil. A compact, neat shrub with blue flowers appearing in late Spring and Summer. Cuttings in mid Summer.

Potentilla fruticosa hybrids are amongst the longest flowered of all shrubs. 'Longacre' will spread over several feet, but grows only 18 inches high. The yellow flowers are carried continuously

Iberis serpervirens

Potentilla

Rock Plants

Alyssum "Gold Dust" *saxatile* 'Compactum' is neat enough to warrant inclusion with masses of yellow flowers in late Spring and early Summer. Propagate by means of cuttings taken in late Spring.

Arabis "Rock Cress", the variety 'Rosabelle' is not so weed-like as the type. Only 6 inches (15 cm) high, it has a cluster of pink flowers in Spring. Cuttings or division.

Arenaria montana, a most attractive mound of bright green foliage 6 inches (15 cm) high

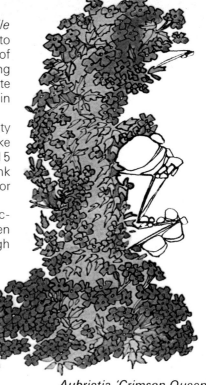

Aubrietia 'Crimson Queen'

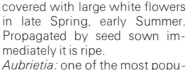

There are so many plants suitable for inclusion in a rock garden it is impossible to describe them all. The following will succeed in most gardens given a well drained soil.

covered with large white flowers in late Spring, early Summer. Propagated by seed sown immediately it is ripe.

Aubrietia: one of the most popular alpine rock plants which spreads into a carpet of colour each Spring with intermittent blossoming continuing through Summer. Particularly suitable for covering slopes, retaining walls, or rich scree.

'Red Carpet' — deep red.
'Dr Mules' — deep rich purple.
'Carnival' — violet.
'Crimson Queen' — crimson.

Propagated by cuttings of young growths produced by plants cut back after flowering.

Campanula "Bell Flower" enjoys almost the same degree of popularity as the Aubrietia and is even more tolerant in the matter of soil and situation.

C. cochlearifolia is a splendid little plant which will creep about in rock crevices or in gritty soil on a ledge, the soft blue flowers open from early Summer into Autumn. *C. warleyensis* has double flowers in a deeper shade of blue.

Chrysanthemum haradjanii has finely divided silvery leaves and is of considerable value for its

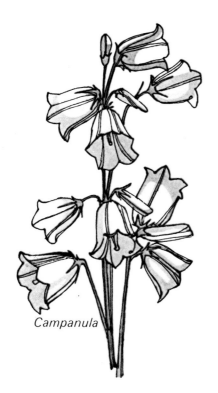

Campanula

Dianthus 'La Bourbille'

Dianthus x arvernensis

foliage. This is enhanced in late Summer by small yellow flowers. Cuttings root readily enough inserted in sharp sand.

Dianthus "Pinks" will thrive in any sunny, well drained soil. Their colour and fragrance is one of Summer's joys.

Dianthus x arvernensis opens a mass of light pink delightfully fragrant flowers in late Spring/early Summer. 'La Bourbille' forms neat tufts of grey leaves, the bright pink fringed flowers are carried on short stems only just clear of the foliage.

Gentiana septemfida is the best general purpose member of a beautiful, but in many cases difficult, family. The clusters of bright blue flowers on 6 inch (15 cm) stems open in mid Summer. Tolerant of both lime and acid soils. Propagate by seed or division.

Geranium napuligerum. A choice plant forming tufts of grey green foliage. Flowers are shell pink with deeper veins and black anthers. Propagate by means of

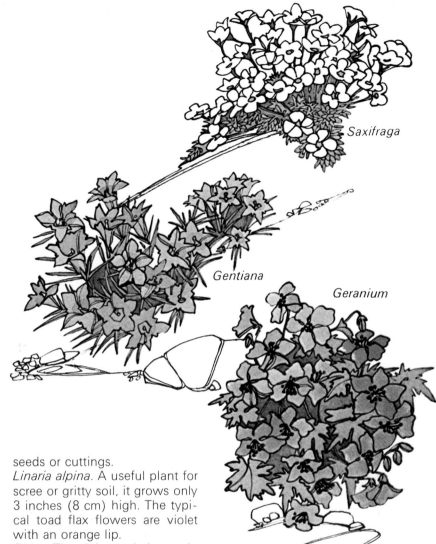

Saxifraga

Gentiana

Geranium

Primula

seeds or cuttings.

Linaria alpina. A useful plant for scree or gritty soil, it grows only 3 inches (8 cm) high. The typical toad flax flowers are violet with an orange lip.

Phlox. The alpine varieties are in most cases prostrate in growth. When the plants are growing freely they flower profusely making a blaze of colour from late Spring to mid Summer. A sandy yet moisture-retentive soil in full sun is ideal.

Forms of *P. douglasii* are excellent value e.g. 'Rose Queen'. Also forms of *P. subulata* extend the flowering season and colour range, 'G. F. Wilson. mauve, and 'Temiscaming' red, purple.

Primula. The alpine species need a degree of attention, but the so called primrose forms are easy and floriferous. Moisture and light shade are all they ask.

'Kinlough Beauty' with soft lilac flowers.

'Lingwood Beauty' with

cherry red flowers.

Saxifraga are to be had in well nigh endless variety. Those listed as 'Encrusted' with silver rosettes prefer a limy gritty soil in full sun, *S. cochlearis* is a good choice in this category.

In the mossy Saxifraga 'Dubarry' with rich crimson flowers is a useful variety, but prefers a place in partial shade and a cool root run.

Thymus drucei is a lovely creeping mat forming plant for growing in paving, rock crevices, or sun baked banks.

'Coccineus' rich crimson, and 'Pink Chintz' are superb.

Water Gardens

Plastic is now a near essential part of everyday gardening life. Nowhere is that impact more apparent than in the water garden. No longer need the would-be pool owner mix and lay huge quantities of concrete, for pre-formed pools have revolutionised pool making.

Both pre-formed and concrete pools require first the removal and disposal of soil from the site. Providing the work is done with care, and there is not a lot of heavy clay in the subsoil, this can in many cases be either turned into a rock outcrop, or spread evenly and thinly over the rest of the garden. In fact, when making a concrete pool I find it best to spread this surplus soil over the area intended to become lawn. During the pre-grass sowing cultivations it is then incorporated into the existing soil.

Mixtures for Base and Sides
1 part good quality cement.
3 parts clean washed gravel graded up to 1 inch (25 mm).
2 parts sharp sand.

For Rendering
1 part cement.
3 parts sand (free of pebbles).

Once the excavations are complete the methods of pool formation diverge. Concrete requires a mould built up with wood, hardboard, etc, any material strong enough to form 'shuttering' by holding the concrete in position until it hardens.

First a layer of broken stone or hardcore is rammed into the base of the hole, about 4 inches (10 cm) is sufficient. Most soils require this base to bind the concrete into a waterproof layer, with the possible exception of heavy clay (1).

The concrete is laid in position on the top of this (2) and allowed to harden for four days before the 'shuttering' for the sides goes into place. Make certain the structure is strengthened sufficiently to take the weight of concrete without bulging (3).

Metal rods or square mesh netting may be used to reinforce both bottom and sides, but it is only necessary on the large pools except maybe at the corners. A week later the 'shuttering' is removed and the pool rubbed down with a breeze block to remove any surplus concrete (4). The whole surface is then rendered to ensure complete water proofing with a mixture of 1 cement, to 3 parts of sand. Use the fine pebble-free sand for the work for these can cause air holes by floating to the top (5).

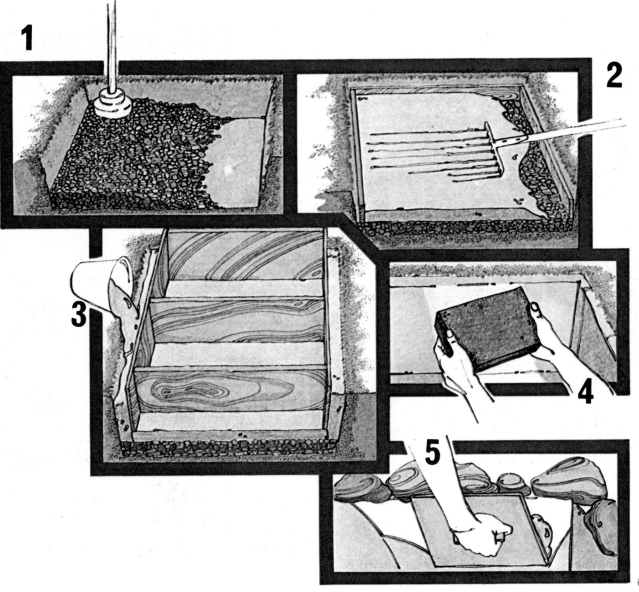

Liner and Pre-formed Pools

On light sand or gravel soils double 'shuttering' may be required to stop the soil falling into the space left for the concrete. This is such a large addition to cost and labour it is advisable to consider pre-formed pools or liners as an alternative.

The 'liner' is fairly simple to install as within broad limits it means digging a hole of the size and shape required, spreading a layer of soft river sand over the bottom (**1**), then lining it with polythene sheeting. Make sure no sharp objects such as stones or roots have been left to puncture the material. The exposed edges should be rammed to a true level all round. Nothing spoils the appearance of a pool more than a vast exposed area of polythene.

Spread the sheets evenly with an overlap of 12–15 inches (30–45 cm) which will ensure a complete seal when the water is run in (**2**). Paving stones laid around the pool edge, or grass sown up to the rim will protect the edges (**3**).

Pools of this description are not really satisfactory as the polythene deteriorates after 4 or 5 years. Sheeting made of Butalene, Vinyl or P.V.C. have the same flexibility, and are laid in the same fashion. They are more durable than polythene but in consequence more expensive.

Pre-formed pools made, as for example, from fibreglass are rigid and may be obtained in a wide variety of shapes, both formal and informal. All are fairly expensive. Installation is a

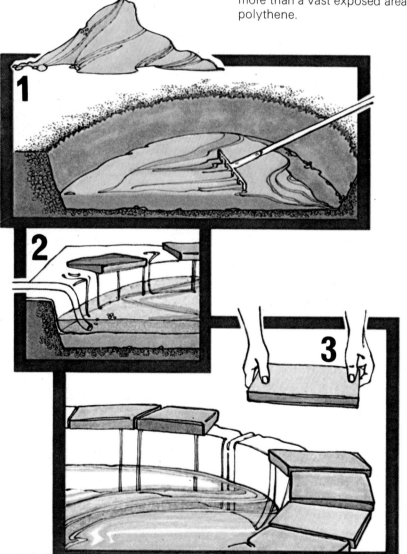

little more involved than with a liner but, compared with a concrete pool, very easy.

Mark out the shape of the pool on the site, dig the hole to match the configurations of the moulded glass fibre, but a little larger. When the excavation is complete line the bottom with soft river sand, place the pool in position and check the level all round. Adjustments can be made by removing a little sand or adding as required. Once the true level is achieved replace and firm the soil but without disturbing the pool. Check all levels when the work is finished or just fill with water which quickly shows up any deficiencies.

Finish off by turfing or paving the exposed edges likely to damage and twist causing seepage of water.

Embellishments such as pumps, water falls, fountains or under-water lighting may be added as desired.

Pools gain in interest if they are stocked with plants and fish. Collections of both may be bought from nurseries which specialise in these. When ordering state the size and depth of the pool. Many aquatic plants grow in a particular depth of water, others are so vigorous they would quickly take over a small pool, so be exact in your description.

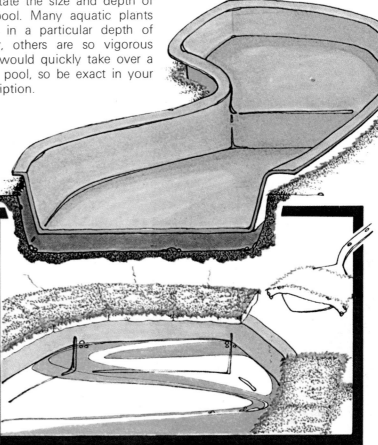

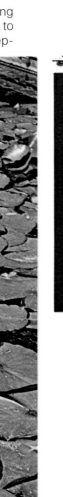

Plants for Water Gardens

Drain the water from the pool, then place the plants in the containers or ledges provided to receive them. The best growing medium is good top spit loam or turf which has been stacked over a year. This is passed through a $\frac{3}{4}$ inch (2 cm) riddle to remove stones and other rubbish. To each 2-gallon bucketful of loam add a handful of bone meal. Bed the plants in this, then top up with straight loam for the last 2 inches (5 cm).

Avoid organic materials such as peat, animal manure and leaf mould which create conditions when rotting which are ruinous to the balance of the pond.

Planting is best done during late Spring/early Summer with water lilies, mid Spring onwards with other aquatics.

To mask the pool edges marginal plants may be included. Caltha, Acorus, the creeping Calla, and Primulas are examples. A bed of soil 6—12 inches (15—30 cm) deep along the inside of the pool margin will do very well.

So called oxygenating plants which help prevent the water becoming foul are not planted but, with a stone attached to the base, just lowered into the pool.

Hardy Water Lilies Suitable for a Small Pool or Tub

'Albatross' white — spread 30 inches (75 cm).

'Aurora' yellow, fades to deep wine red — spread 24 inches (60 cm).

'Sunrise' yellow and scented — 36 inches (90 cm).

There are many more to choose from in the specialist growers' lists.

'Ellisiana' garnet red — spread 30 inches (75 cm).

'Firecrest' deep pink — spread 24—30 inches (60—75 cm).

'Purpurata' rosy crimson — speckled white — 24 inches (60 cm).

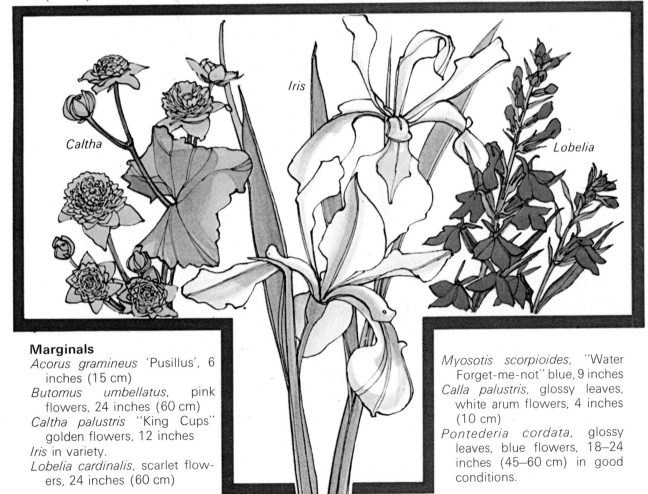

Marginals

Acorus gramineus 'Pusillus', 6 inches (15 cm)

Butomus umbellatus, pink flowers, 24 inches (60 cm)

Caltha palustris "King Cups" golden flowers, 12 inches

Iris in variety.

Lobelia cardinalis, scarlet flowers, 24 inches (60 cm)

Myosotis scorpioides, "Water Forget-me-not" blue, 9 inches

Calla palustris, glossy leaves, white arum flowers, 4 inches (10 cm)

Pontederia cordata, glossy leaves, blue flowers, 18—24 inches (45—60 cm) in good conditions.

Bulbs

Bulb Culture Indoors

The most popular bulbs for forcing are hyacinths, narcissus and tulips.

Plant up the bulbs from early to mid Autumn. Where possible choose the bulbs which have been specially prepared for early flowering.

Bulb fibre or balanced compost provides the correct moisture-holding material without becoming stagnant if a few pieces of charcoal are mixed in at planting time.

Bowls without drainage holes are perfectly satisfactory provided watering is done carefully. When potting is complete the finished level of the compost should be half an inch (6 mm) below the rim of the pot to allow for watering.

Stand the bulbs in a cool dark place for 8–10 weeks so that a good strong root system is formed. Alternatively dig a hole on the north side of the house, stand the pots in that and cover with sand, peat or ashes. A constant, cool temperature over a period of weeks is essential at this stage.

Outdoors the bulbs should need little attention in regard to watering; inside check to see they are moist enough once a fortnight. When the roots are formed and leaf tips showing move the bowls into a cool room for a fortnight, by which time they will take the higher temperature in the living room to bring on the flowers. High temperatures mean dry atmosphere so stand the bowls on a tray of moist sand or pebbles to restore the right degree of humidity.

Botanically, bulbs are modified buds; in the garden it is a term which covers all swollen underground stems, corms, tubers, even rhizomes. Indispensable for garden display, bulbs, starting with snowdrops, anticipate Spring, gladiolus add a tropical brilliance to the Summer, while the hardy cyclamen provide marbled foliage as a background to the elegant flowers in late Autumn.

Use bulbs naturalised in grass, to fill spaces down the borders, or in bowls in the house. Indeed, it is this versatility which makes them so useful in the garden.

Bulbs in the Garden

Allium moly 12 inches (30 cm) high, leaves grey, flowers bright yellow during early Summer. Plant in a well drained border fully exposed to the sun.

Alstroemeria Ligtu hybrids are useful in the garden and as cut flowers. The colour range is wide — orange, flame and deep red predominating. 24 inches (60 cm) high.

Pot grown tubers should be planted in light sandy soil in mid Spring 6 inches (15 cm) deep, 12 inches (30 cm) apart. Alternatively, seed may be sown in deep boxes filled with John Innes compost in early Spring.

Chionodoxa "Glory of the Snow" make a useful Spring display when used as an underplanting for Summer flowering shrubs. Any reasonably fertile soil should prove suitable. Seed is produced in abundance and can be sown in seed compost, grown on for a year, then planted out to flower two years later. Alternatively plant mature bulbs in the Autumn.

Colchicum erroneously referred to as the autumn crocus are beautiful Autumn flowering bulbs. The leaves are produced in the normal way during early Spring then die away until the goblet-shaped flowers appear from the bare earth during early Autumn.

Plant the bulbs 3—4 inches (8—10 cm) deep during late Summer in the shrub border or rough grassland. *C. speciosum* — mauve. The white form is particularly attractive. 12 inches (30 cm) high.

Crocus Deservedly ranked amongst the most popular bulbous plants. They need a well drained, sunny position to give of their best, although will succeed in most soils including clay. They are eminently suitable for underplanting with dwarf shrubs in the rock garden, while the stronger growing species will naturalise in grass so long as mowing is not carried out until the leaves die back. Planting should be done in Summer whenever the corms are available for the Autumn and Spring flowering species.

Mice can be troublesome, eating the corms during the Winter; when this is liable to be a problem grow the corms in pots then plant out when almost in flower.

Crocus chrysanthus, in all its forms for growing in pots or the open garden. 'Blue Pearl' — pale blue. 'E. A. Bowles' yellow. 'Snow Bunting' — white. 'Zwanenburg Bronze' — bronze and yellow are well tried favourites.

Crocus speciosus is a useful, late Autumn flowering variety — lilac blue blossoms with bright anthers.

Crocus tomasinianus becomes almost weedlike in some gardens, but established mixed forms are a joy to look at in late Winter. Pale lavender to deep purple.

Cyclamen neapolitanum is a hardy species which has attractively marbled leaves surmounted by dainty pale pink or mauve flowers in early Autumn.

Tulip   Narcissus   Gladiolus

Outdoor Bulbs 2

Plants grown from seed sown in mid Winter should flower two years later.

Eranthis hyemalis. The popular winter aconite will contentedly naturalise itself when soil conditions are suitable. A well drained yet moisture retentive alkaline loam fills the requirements.

Plant the tubers in early Autumn about an inch (2–3 cm) deep. Division of the tubers or seed sown immediately it is ripe are suitable methods of propagation.

Galanthus. The delicate, pendent white flowers of the snowdrops which anticipate Spring in the garden. Nearly all garden soils seem to suit galanthus, but moist loams in light shade are the best.

Stock may be increased by sowing seed immediately it is ripe or division of established groups as soon as the flowers fade.

Dry bulbs should be planted on receipt, never stored, or they are difficult to establish.

Two forms of *G. nivalis* are to be recommended: 'Flore Plena' with double flowers, or 'S. Arnott' superbly elegant.

Gladioli are best suited with a well drained soil and a place in full sun. A dressing of complete fertilizer should be raked into the soil a fortnight before planting, 2 oz per square yard (70 g/m²) is sufficient.

On light soils plant the corms 4–6 inches (10–12 cm) deep. When the soil is cold or inclined to be wet start the corms into growth on a bed of moist peat under glass. For planting take out a trench 4 inches (10 cm) deep, put a layer of sharp sand in the bottom and press the corms into this.

After flowering lift the corms as the foliage starts to yellow and hang up to dry in a light airy shed. Remove soil and foliage before storing the corms in shallow trays.

Varieties are: Large Flowered 'Flowersong' – yellow; 'A. Schweitzer' – salmon. Primulinus are slightly smaller at 15–36 inches (38–90 cm) and they make useful cut flowers; 'R. Unwin' – velvet crimson; 'Rosy Maid' – apricot.

Miniatures range in height between 18–36 inches (45–90 cm) but frequently have frilled flowers; 'Bo Peep' – apricot; 'Zenith' – pink.

Butterfly hybrids will grow 4 ft (1·2 m) high and are very popular as they are eminently suitable for cutting: 'Mme Butterfly' – shell pink; 'Walt Disney' – yellow.

Hyacinthus The species from which the modern varieties used so extensively for forcing have been bred is *H. orientalis*.

Bulbs to be flowered outdoors in the garden are planted in the Autumn 4 inches (10 cm) deep, 6 inches (15 cm) apart. The soil must be well prepared, clear of weeds and well drained.

Suitable varieties include: 'City of Haarlam' – yellow; 'Jan Bos' – cerise pink; and 'Bismark' – blue.

Iris Bulbous species prefer a light, well drained soil and a position in full sun. Heavy soils may be made lighter by working in heavy dressings of lime chippings. Plant the bulbs 2 inches (5 cm) deep in early Autumn; as the flowers fade work in a dressing of fish meal or similar fertilizer. Species *Iris danfordiae* – yellow
Iris histrioides – blue
Iris reticulata vars. – blue purple.

Muscari Grape hyacinths are most accommodating bulbs growing in any well drained soil.

Plant 2 inches (5 cm) deep in late Summer, early Autumn.

Species *M. botryoides* – blue, 8 inches (20 cm). *M. moschatum* – pale purple, fading, 9 inches (23 cm). *M. tubergenianum* – pale blue, 8 inches.

Narcissus There can surely be no more popular Spring flower. From the dwarf species to the taller modern hybrids they offer a quality of bloom which is unsurpassed.

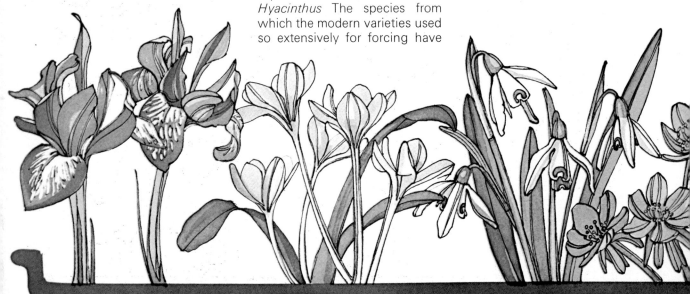

Iris   *Colchicum*   *Galanthus*   *Eranthis hyemar*

The bulbs can be grown in groups amongst shrubs, naturalised in grass, in pots under glass, or in the case of the miniature species amongst the alpines in the rock garden.

A deep, rich, well drained yet moisture retentive soil suits most narcissus. Bulbs should not be planted into land which has been freshly manured or it causes soft rot. Plant in late Summer/early Autumn. Depth of planting varies according to variety, but 3–4 times the height of the bulb is a rough guide.

A dressing of complete fertilizer each year just as growth commences will keep the bulbs in good flowering condition.

Species *N. asturiensis*, a neat trumpet flower on 3 inch (8 cm) stems in late Winter is suitable for the well drained pockets in the rock garden.

N. bulbocodium — "Hoop Petticoat Narcissus" is offered in many varieties. The deep trumpets, fringed with narrow petals, open in late Winter.

N. cyclamineus has some of the best varieties for the small garden. The type plant has rich gold flowers on 8 inch (20 cm) stems, the petals swept back.

'Peeping Tom', 'March Sunshine' and 'February Gold' are useful cyclamineus hybrids.

The choice in garden varieties must be personal, but 'Foresight'—yellow cup, cream petals; 'Mount Hood' — all white; 'King Alfred' — yellow self; and 'Scarlet Elegance' — orange cup, are a small selection.

Scilla make such a glorious blue contrast to the daffodils and are so easy to grow they must be included in the bulb garden as the near perfect beginners' plant.

Any good garden soil suits them.

S. bifolia with deep blue flowers on 6 inch stems (15 cm).

S. siberica flowers brilliant blue, 6 inches high (15 cm).

Plant the bulbs 2 inches (5 cm) deep as ground cover in partial shade or full sun during early Autumn.

Tulipa Another of the well nigh indispensable plants for Spring bedding, or to provide early colour in the rock garden. Though the bulbs can be almost guaranteed to produce a flower the first Spring after planting, to bloom in subsequent years a well drained soil and a position in full sun is vital.

For bedding work bulbs are planted 4–6 inches (10–12 cm) during late Autumn into soil which has been cultivated to a depth of 12–15 inches (30–38 cm).

A dressing of lime is essential if the soil is at all acid.

Spacing depends on the effect required, but 4–6 inches (10–15 cm) is usual.

Tulips are divided into groups — Single or double early, Mendel, Darwin, Triumph, Lily Flowered, Cottage, Parrot, Lates, and Species.

'Keizerskroon' — yellow/red. 12 inches (30 cm). Mid Spring.

'Merechal Niel' — yellow. 15 inches (38 cm). Mid Spring.

'Krelages Triumph' — Dark red, edged yellow. 18 inches (45 cm). Late Spring.

'Edith Eddy' — red, edged white. 20 inches (50 cm). Mid Spring.

'Apeldoorn', rich red. 18 inches (45 cm). Mid Spring.

'Scarlet O'Hara', scarlet. 24 inches (60 cm). Late Spring.

'China Pink', pink. 20 inches (50 cm). Mid Spring.

'Dillenburg', deep orange. 28 inches (70 cm). Late Spring.

'Parrot', orange red. 18 inches (38 cm). Mid Spring.

'Brilliant Fire', red. 20 inches (50 cm). Mid Spring.

Species include:

T. 'fosteriana', bright red.

T. 'greigii', orange scarlet flowers, purple veined leaves.

T. 'kaufmanniana' "Water Lily Tulip", white flowers, flushed red.

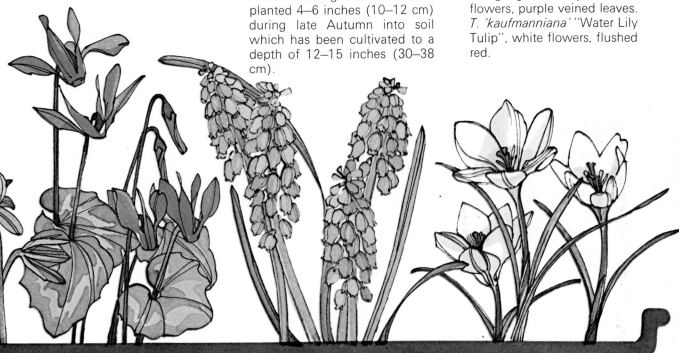

Cyclamen neapolitanum   *Muscari*   *Crocus*

Annuals and Biennials

Both groups contribute enormously to the beauty of our gardens, especially during the Summer months.

Annuals are capable of completing their life cycle in a single year — growing, flowering, ripening seed. They may be subdivided to suit the gardeners' convenience into two groups: *hardy*, those which may be sown direct where they are to flower (Marigolds are an example); *half hardy*, those which need the protection of a greenhouse until fear of frost has passed (Asters are typical of this group).

Biennials need two years to complete their life cycle. Growth the first year, flowering and seed ripening the next. This group are an essential part of the spring scene. Wallflowers are grown as a hardy biennial.

Hardy Annuals

The soil for annuals should not be too rich otherwise the plants run to leaf growth instead of flowers. Dig the bed over in the Autumn, working in at the same time a light dressing of well rotted compost. This ensures a friable, moisture-retentive seed bed which enables the seedlings to grow away strongly. No further fertilizer should be required, but if the soil is known to be in poor condition a dusting of fish meal at 2 oz per square yard (70 g/m²) may be worked in a fortnight before sowing.

Some annuals if sown during early Autumn will flower earlier and over a longer period than when sown during mid to late Spring. Sweet Peas are the best example — sown in Autumn, flowering is at least ten days in advance of those sown in late Winter. Spring sowing should take place immediately the soil is warm enough to encourage the seed to germinate.

Common causes of seed failing to germinate are, sowing too early when the soil is too cold and wet, and sowing too deeply.

Draw shallow drills across the bed, sow the seed in these evenly along the rows, *see right*. Fine seed may be mixed with dry sand to help even distribution; this saves time-consuming hand weeding later. Sometimes cold weather after germination causes a check to growth — help the plants to get over this with a dilute nitrogen liquid feed.

The final spacing of the seedlings depends on the ultimate height, 4 inches (10 cm) for dwarf varieties, up to 15 inches (38 cm) for vigorous plants like clarkia or lavatera.

Keep the bed weed-free and make sure the plants are never seriously short of moisture. A sprinkling overhead with a can after a hot day wonderfully refreshes tired annuals.

Blackfly and greenfly are sometimes a problem but can be controlled without difficulty by one or two sprays with a systemic insecticide.

Well grown annuals do not as a rule need support, but occasionally after a Summer gale a few judiciously placed twiggy branches may be necessary.

75

Annuals: Select List

Hardy Annuals

Alyssum 'Little Dorrit' 4 inches (10 cm) high, white flowers. Makes a useful edge to the rose border when mixed with Viola.

Calendula The ever popular marigold once planted will appear year after year from self-sown seedlings. Average about 15 inches (38 cm). Varieties: 'Orange King' with double orange flowers, 'Lemon Queen' double lemon flowers, and 'Radio' deep rich orange.

Candytuft will make brilliant patches of colour sown in groups down the borders. To achieve the best display thin to about 6 inches (15 cm) apart. 'Dwarf Fairy Mixed' produces a richly varied range of colours. 6 inches (15 cm) high.

Clarkia elegans May be sown in early Autumn or late Spring. The full double flowers are carried on slender spikes throughout the Summer. Excellent cut flower. *Clarkia elegans* 'Double Mixed' 24 inches (60 cm) high.

Cornflower The double flowered strains are good for garden display and cutting. Light soils are most suitable, the seedlings being thinned to 9 inches (23 cm) apart after germination. 'Tall Double Mixed' are useful back of the border plants and for cutting. 30 inches (75 cm) high. For the small garden 'Dwarf Double Mixed' 12 inches (30 cm) high.

Eschscholzia The brightly coloured Californian poppy is best grown as a hardy annual because it resents being transplanted. 'Ballerina' gives a wide range of colours ranging from yellow to scarlet 10 inches (25 cm) high. 'Miniature Primrose' a delicately formed pale yellow poppy, useful in rock or tiny borders, 5 inches (13 cm) high.

Godetia The large showy flowers carried over a long period are useful as cut bloom. 'Tall Double Mixed' 2 ft (60 cm). 'Dwarf Mixed' 10 inches (25 cm). 'Azalea Flowered' 12–14 inches (30–35 cm) high.

Helichrysum The long flowering season makes this a most useful annual. Everlasting stems are so stiff and erect they rarely need staking. Can be cut and dried for winter decoration. 'Dwarf Spangled Mixture' 14 inches (35 cm) high.

Larkspur One of the earliest annuals to flower. The finely divided foliage makes a suitable foil to the spikes of double flowers. Tall 'Stock Flowered' mixed 3 ft (90 cm) high.

Lavatera "Mallow" A most impressive sight when the tall bushy plants are embellished with large pink trumpet shaped flowers. Because the plants are tall and spreading allow 15 inches (38 cm) spacing each way, 30 inches (75 cm) high.

Limnanthes douglasii A marvellously free flowering annual excellent for bees, well named "Foam of the Meadow". May also be grown as a pot plant. The flowers are yellow, edged with white, and once planted will continue to flower for several years from self sown seedlings.

Nigella "Love in a Mist" may be sown outdoors in early Autumn, but on colder soils it is advisable to wait until late Spring. The feathery foliage and cornflower like flowers add a touch of elegance to the borders.

'Miss Jekyll', clear blue, 18 inches (45 cm) high.

'Jewel Mixture', pink/blue, 15 inches (38 cm) high.

Half Hardy Annuals

Continuous cropping with bedding plants will eventually impoverish the soil. Fork the bed over in Autumn, incorporating compost, bone meal, or seaweed fertilizer at the same time. This helps to maintain soil struc-

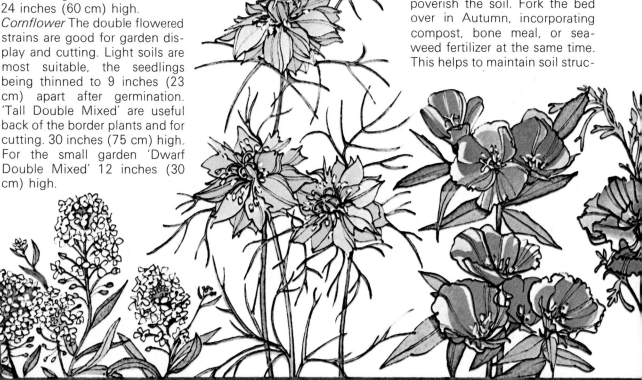

Alyssum   *Nigella*   *Godetia*

ture which would otherwise be lost.

Seed is sown under glass into a suitable seed compost (see chapter on propagation) from late Winter to mid Spring depending on the species being handled.

Prick off the seedlings into pots or seed trays immediately they are large enough to handle. Spaced at 28 or 35 to a standard tray filled with John Innes No. 1 compost, or peat based compost.

Keep the boxes watered and in a light airy greenhouse. Harden off in frames for 10–14 days before planting out in their flowering position in late Spring.

Weed control, dead heading, watering and feeding should be attended to as required. Should the plants check after planting, a dilute liquid feed will assist recovery.

Ageratum 'Blue Blazer', 5 inches (13 cm), makes an attractive edging to a bed of *Antirrhinum* 'Coronette' with flowers of bronze, deep red, yellow and pink.

Antirrhinum 'Floral Cluster' is outstanding value. They can be grown true to colour which makes planning a bedding

scheme so much easier. 12 inches (30 cm) high.

Asters unfortunately are liable to infection with wilt disease. When a soil is suspect grow only resistant varieties. The dwarf 'Milady Rose' and 'Milady Blue' are noteworthy both for bedding and pot work. 10 inches (25 cm) high. 'Ostrich Plume' with feathery heads of bloom is taller at 18 inches (45 cm).

African Marigolds bring an extravagant carnival atmosphere to the garden. Planted close enough so the plants touch, the mass of flowers presents an unbroken carpet of colour. Sow the seed in Spring under glass for planting out early Summer.

Varieties include: 'Gold Galore', 4 inches (10 cm), flowers rich gold, full double. 'Red and Gold Hybrids', 24 inches (60 cm), red and gold flowers. 'Petite Harmony', 6 inches (15 cm), gold with mahogany guard petals.

Lobelia Almost indispensable as an edging plant, forming mounds of flowers only 4 or 5 inches (10–12 cm) high. Sow in early Spring under glass but do not cover the seed. 'Cambridge Blue' and 'Mrs Clibran' are good bright coloured varieties.

For hanging baskets blue or red 'Cascade'.

Petunia: Few garden flowers have been so improved in quality by selective breeding. For bedding work, window boxes or hanging baskets, because of their wide range of colours, they

are amongst the most useful of all annuals. The (F. I.) Hybrid varieties offer a longer flowering season and wider colour range.

Sow the seed in early Spring. Pelleted seed may be pressed one at a time into the surface of the compost so the sowing depth and spacing can be judged exactly.

Varieties:
  'Red Cap' – red scarlet.
  'Plum Crazy' – pink, lavender, plum.
  'Blue Skies' – light blue.

Eschscholzia   Helichrysum   Lobelia   Sweet Peas

Select List 2

Salvia are usually grown as half hardy annuals. They are one of the most vivid and vibrant coloured of all popular bedding plants.

Sow the seed in early Spring under glass. A high temperature 65°F (18°C) is required to ensure even germination. Prick out individually into peat pots when large enough to handle. Harden off for 10–14 days in a cold frame before planting out in a sunny position during late Spring early Summer.

Varieties:

'Blaze of Fire', 12 inches (30 cm).

'Early Bird', 10 inches (25 cm) earliest to bloom.

Stocks One of the most fragrant of all bedding plants. A massed planting of stocks in full bloom is a picture to delight the eye, the colour and fragrance adds immeasurably to the garden scene. The 100% double varieties are to be preferred. The compact well furnished spikes of flowers are also good for cutting.

Seed can be sown in early Summer, and the plants are grown on in pots to flower under glass during late Autumn. Normal sowing time for bedding out is early Spring.

100% Double stocks should be grown under slightly cooler conditions so the single flowered seedlings which have dark green leaves can be removed, leaving only the pale green leaved plants to produce full double flowers.

Varieties: 100% "Double Bedding", 15–18 inches (38–45 cm). "Double Ten Week", 12 inches (30 cm).

Sweet Peas Seed may be sown under a cold frame or cloche for early flowering. Sow two seeds to a peat pot, using John Innes No. 1 Compost. Allow three days to pass, then give all the pots a thorough soaking. Alternatively, seed may be sown under glass in early Spring after allowing the seed to soak overnight in tepid water — this encourages rapid germination.

To ensure continuity of flowering a further sowing may be made direct into the open ground 4–6 weeks later.

Sweet peas are greedy feeders, so prepare the soil well in advance. Open up a trench 24 inches (60 cm) deep by 3 ft (90 cm) across. This is wide enough to accommodate a double row of plants. Fork a heavy dressing of manure into the trench bottom, then as the soil is replaced mix in additional manure. Leave to settle over Winter before planting in Spring. The same soil preparation is required if the peas are grown on tripods or wigwams.

Support the plants as they grow on canes, string nets or sticks.

Varieties: The Spencer varieties in mixed colours are excellent. For those who prefer lower growing sweet peas, 'Jet Set' are very good.

Petunia   *Antirrhinum*   *Cornflower*

Biennials

These include so many of the best-known garden flowers — sweet william, wallflower, double daisy and canterbury bell are examples. They are usually sown outdoors from late Spring to mid Summer.

Choose a sheltered, slightly shaded border as the nursery seed bed. The soil should be in good condition but not too rich.

Apply a dressing of superphosphate 1 oz per square yard (35 g/m²) 10 days before sowing.

Sow the seed in drills 6 inches (15 cm) apart, not too thickly or the young plants become overcrowded before they can be moved.

Line out 6 inches (15 cm) apart when large enough to handle in a bed where they can grow on until early Autumn when they are transferred to their flowering position. At no time from seed to flowering should the plants be short of water.

Canterbury Bell An old traditional cottage garden favourite. The 'Cup and Saucer' varieties are so frequently depicted against a background of whitewashed walls and thatched roof.

Seeds are sown during late Spring/early Summer in a sheltered, shady border in drills $\frac{1}{2}$ inch (6 mm) deep. They are transferred to flowering positions in early Autumn.

Varieties: 'Dwarf Bedding' or 'Bells of Holland mixture' — useful for the small garden at 15–18 inches (38–45 cm) high. 'Cup and Saucer' (Calycanthema) mixed — in shades of blue, lavender and pink. 30 inches (75 cm) high.

Cheiranthus x allionii "Siberian Wallflower". Usually grown as a biennial, though it is in truth a perennial, the flowers are vividly colourful and sweetly scented. Seed may be sown in early Summer in a partially shaded border in drills 2 inches (5 cm) apart $\frac{1}{4}$ inch (3 mm) deep.

A dressing of lime worked into the soil both in the nursery and flowering position may help to prevent club root fungus.

When large enough to handle prick the young plants out 6 inches (15 cm) apart, and at the same time nip off the base of the tap root to encourage fibrous root formation. When the seedlings have grown to 6 inches (15 cm) or so nip out the growing tip to promote side growths.

Plant out in flowering positions in Autumn, spacing them 12 inches (30 cm) apart.

Varieties:
'Golden Bedder' — 15 inches (38 cm).
C. cheiri — the ever popular wallflower needs a slightly longer growing season than its Siberian counterpart, but cultivations are the same.
'Fire King' — rich scarlet.
'Cloth of Gold'.
'Vulcan' — deep red.
'Ruby Gem' — ruby violet.

Lunaria "Honesty — Satin Flower". Though the purple or white tend to be somewhat nondescript, the silvery seed pods are ornamental and much sought after by flower arrangers.

Seed is sown outdoors in early Summer, then when large enough the seedlings are pricked out to grow on for planting up in early Autumn.

Grow the purple and white mixture, even the form with variegated foliage.

Myosotis "Forget-me-not". Sow in late Spring/early Summer into a frame. Prick off when large enough to handle, and then plant up in flowering positions during early Autumn. They flower in Spring and look well planted with dark red tulips.

Varieties:
'Blue Bouquet', 15 inches (38 cm).
'Royal Blue', 12 inches (30 cm).

Lunaria   Myosotis   Cheiranthus allionii

Greenhouses

A greenhouse is a valuable gardening aid giving the gardener a degree of control over growing conditions impossible to achieve outdoors. Temperature, humidity, even light, can all be adjusted to suit a particular plant's needs, but with rapidly escalating fuel costs it can be an expensive hobby. The beginner would be well advised to start with an unheated house, then make additions to the system as the need arises.

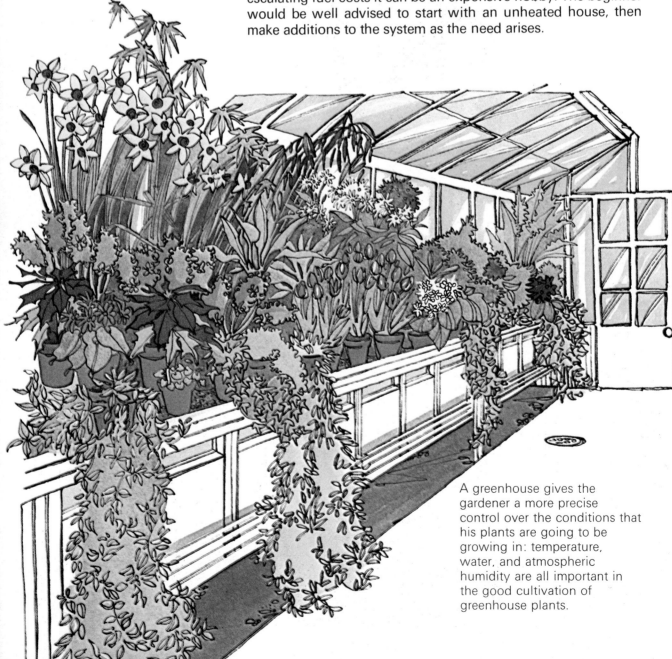

A greenhouse gives the gardener a more precise control over the conditions that his plants are going to be growing in: temperature, water, and atmospheric humidity are all important in the good cultivation of greenhouse plants.

Choosing one greenhouse from the many different types on offer can in itself be a problem. Wood or metal?

Metal frameworks can be narrower than wood, so in theory let in more light. They need less maintenance as the surface areas are treated (insist on this) with an anti-corrosive material. On the debit side, achieving a complete seal and preventing drip is more difficult than in a wooden house.

Wooden frameworks are becoming increasingly expensive, and need treating with a preservative every two years. They do however lose heat less rapidly, blend into the landscape better than metal, and are still the most popular.

Siting of the greenhouse should be adjusted so as to get the maximum benefit from sunlight, particularly important in Winter when the light intensity is low.

Lean-to greenhouses should be on a south wall, and span greenhouses should be constructed in a position where their longest side runs east to west.

Greenhouses are classified as follows:

Span roof, when both sides of the roof slope equally.

Hip span, when the roof on one side comes much nearer to ground level than the other.

Lean-to, when the roof slopes in one direction only, the back being formed by a vertical wall.

Although pelargoniums are easily cultivated plants they do offer the beginner in particular a magnificent display with very little effort and the greenhouse enables him to grow a much wider range of colour and foliage interest to combine with the flamboyance of the pelargoniums.

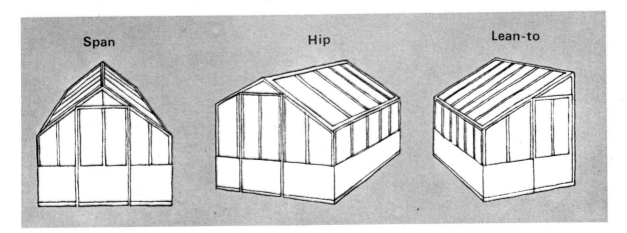

Span   **Hip**   **Lean-to**

Getting the Best from your Greenhouse

Foundations and Walls

These may be of concrete as materials are readily available and it makes a strong retentive wall. Bricks are also easy to obtain and make a strong wall if the joints are kept pointed, but not so easy to keep clean as concrete. Breeze blocks may also be used. Wood is the best insulating material of the four, thickness for thickness, but unless it is treated with a preserving material it rots fairly quickly.

Greenhouses may, of course, be glazed to soil level, a practice adopted if plants, for example tomatoes, are to be cultivated in beds made up on the floor of the house. The merit of a framework fitted on vertical walls is that it gives more head room and is cheaper to heat than a glass to ground structure. A compromise would be to have the south side glass to ground, the north side on a 3 ft (90 cm) brick, breeze block or concrete wall.

All foundations, even of a glass to ground structure, must be laid to a true level, or erecting the house becomes extremely difficult.

Ventilation

Ventilation must be adjusted to provide a free flow of air but devoid of draughts, so the atmosphere inside the greenhouse can be kept fresh and buoyant.

Ventilators fixed along the ridge and at ground level provide a good air flow, and should be easy to operate and maintain.

On windy days ventilate only on the leeward side. Never ventilate when frosty. Avoid extremes of temperature by adjusting the air flow according to prevailing weather conditions.

Never cement the whole floor of a greenhouse, only the pathway. Bare earth under a staging enables the gardener to maintain a humid, growing atmosphere better than is possible with all concrete.

Staging makes maintenance easier by raising the plants to a convenient height. The plants in pots are displayed to better advantage. A suitable height would be 36–42 inches (90–110 cm), and width a comfortable arm reach, approximately 42 inches (110 cm).

A gap of 6–8 inches (15–20 cm) is left between the side of the greenhouse and the back of the staging to allow free air circulation, otherwise 'dead' patches occur which encourage disease.

Supports should be placed at 4–5 ft (1·2–1·5 m) intervals; be sure they are strong enough to take the weight placed on them.

A perfectly adequate staging can be made from angle iron, cut to length then drilled for bolting together. Supports can be made from lengths of gas pipe or thick angle clamped to cross pieces for rigidity. The bed of the staging may be of corrugated asbestos or the traditional wooden slats which allow free air circulation. When using asbestos, a layer of pebbles should be laid on top for the pots to stand in.

The area beneath the staging need not be dead ground. Use it for forcing rhubarb, mushrooms, or growing ferns, begonia, tradescantia etc.

Heating

The type of unit installed depends on what the gardener can afford.

Solid fuel (coal or coke) demands a lot of attention but is competitive in price with both oil and electricity.

Paraffin heaters are less demanding but not so efficient, and must be cleaned regularly or fumes may kill the plants.

Oil fired units are expensive to install, require outdoor storage tanks, but are easy to maintain and are efficient.

Both gas and electricity are clean, efficient, easily controlled methods of heating a greenhouse, but expensive. Electricity is the most versatile; space and soil heating, mist propagation units, soil sterilization, automatic watering, ventilation and even pest control are all possible. For the busy man who can afford it, electricity, if one disregards, power cuts, is the ideal form of heating.

Temperature can only be controlled within the limits of the heating system installed. The beginner should aim to maintain the greenhouse at a minimum of 45°F (7°C) and work on from there.

Remember that for every 10°F (5·5°C) rise in temperature your heating costs could double or even treble. Lining the greenhouse with polythene will help considerably to cut heating costs.

Shading

Shading may be necessary from mid Spring onwards. Left unshaded, the heat can very quickly rise to a level which is harmful to the plants inside.

Slatted or cotton blinds are ideal but expensive and, unless automated, have to be raised and lowered by hand according to the weather.

Chemical dye, once sprayed on the glass, is there for the Summer.

Green polythene pinned on inside the glass is effective, but once in place is difficult to remove until the Autumn without making heavy demands on the gardener's time.

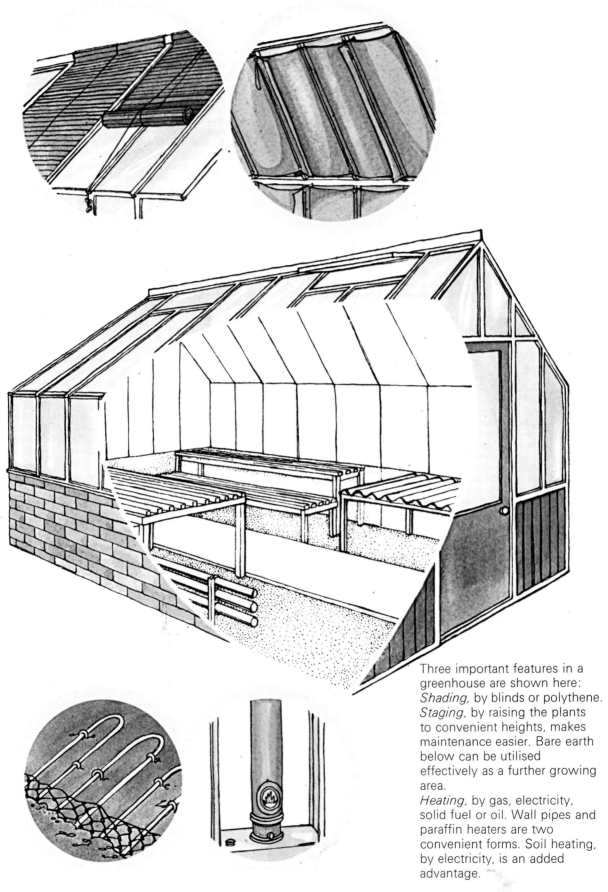

Three important features in a
greenhouse are shown here:
Shading, by blinds or polythene.
Staging, by raising the plants
to convenient heights, makes
maintenance easier. Bare earth
below can be utilised
effectively as a further growing
area.
Heating, by gas, electricity,
solid fuel or oil. Wall pipes and
paraffin heaters are two
convenient forms. Soil heating,
by electricity, is an added
advantage.

Greenhouse Routines

In Spring and Summer check that:

a. All the plants are well watered; not just the surface of the compost but the whole of the pot evenly moist.

b. No pests or diseases are in evidence.

c. Shading and ventilation are adequate depending on the weather.

Remember

More plants are killed by over- than under-watering, so when in doubt do not water.

In Winter check daily to make sure the heating is functioning. Reduce watering and ventilation to a minimum.

By damping down the paths during the growing season a buoyant humid atmosphere is maintained, and the overall internal temperature reduced.

Clean the greenhouse down with a good disinfectant at least once a year.

Make sure the water tank, glass, gutters, and brick, stone or woodwork are clean, free from cracks or decay which could form a breeding ground for pests.

Pots and boxes should be scrubbed clean before storing.

Composts used for potting and seed sowing should be free from pests, diseases and weeds.

When crops are planted direct

into the floor of the house, tomatoes, lettuce etc, sterilize or change the soil every two years, or a build-up of pests and diseases is inevitable.

Frames

Frames are useful as an alternative or supplementary aid to the greenhouse. Those which take a Dutch light are the most useful size. The English or pit light really needs two people to lift it.

They are useful for hardening off seedlings raised in the glass house; for protecting young plants, and growing early salads; or for summer crops, melon, cucumber, courgettes.

Tender plants such as chrysanthemums, fuchsia etc, can be housed in them provided they are kept frost-free.

Fitted with soil-warming cables they can be used for raising seeds or cuttings, and for forcing early vegetables.

Below:
Both chrysanthemums and fuchsias can be carried over the difficult period during the Winter until all fear of frost has gone and then they can be transferred to the open garden. One of the advantages of having a heated frame is to enable the gardener to cultivate plants which would otherwise be impossible in our climate.

Vegetables

Nowhere in the garden is the value of thorough soil cultivation more apparent than in the vegetable garden. Rewards are in proportion to the amount of effort expended.

Double digging, especially if the land being brought into cultivation is old pasture or very weed-infested, is essential. The whole plot need not be double dug the first year but spread out over the four-year rotation, a quarter section a year; the remainder may be single trenched. Work in a heavy dressing of manure or compost with the double digging – in the Autumn if the soil is heavy – in the Spring if the soil is light sand.

Crop rotation (see diagram) has several advantages.

Full use is made of fertilizer and plant residues. Some vegetables, e.g. lettuce or cabbage, need nitrogen to produce leaf growth so they follow legumes (peas, beans) which have special nodules on the root which actually fix nitrogen.

The risk of carrying on disease is very much reduced, eel worm on potatoes and club root of brassica are just two examples.

Rotation helps to clear the ground of weeds. Potato and brassica are 'clearing' crops. They follow carrots and peas which are not easy to keep weed-free. A place can be set aside across one side of the vegetable garden for herbs, rhubarb, or other crops which hold the ground for several years.

A greenhouse or frame, both if the garden will support them, are invaluable for raising seedlings or protecting crops which give a better return under cover, such as tomatoes. Cloches are also a help in getting early crops.

Intercropping
To make full use of the space where possible, quick maturing salad vegetables may be sown between slower growing crops. Examples would be lettuce be-

1st year	2nd year	3rd year	4th year

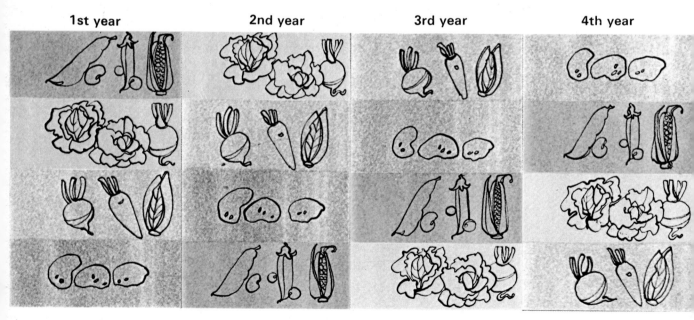

tween main crop peas, radish as an indicator for parsnips, short horn carrot between onions.

No plot in the vegetable garden should be vacant for long during the growing season. Early potatoes may be followed by leeks or lettuce; early peas by a crop of spring cabbage; over-wintering cabbage by sweet corn. When no catch crop suggests itself sow green manure for digging in to rot and act as a soil conditioner.

Green Manure. Vetches and annual lupins are sometimes used, but most often mustard or rape. Mustard sown at 1 oz per 8 square yards (35 g/8 m²). Rape 1 oz per 10 square yards (35 g/10 m²) any time between early Spring and late Summer.

Dig in just before the plants flower if possible, adding a dusting of high nitrogen fertilizer to help quicken the rotting down process, though this is not essential.

One of the prime requirements of a well run vegetable garden is that it should provide a succession of vegetables all the year. Once peas start to crop they should continue until late Autumn. There should be a continuous supply of lettuce throughout the Summer. This is achieved by sowing under cloches in early Autumn, then in Spring sowing an 8 ft (2·4 m) row every ten days; each short row should give 10 good heads. Stagger the sowing of cauliflowers, beetroots and carrots so that they crop over a period of weeks and not all at once.

Above all keep the garden clean. Do not leave heaps of rotting vegetation lying about, compost them. Burn all disease or pest infected plants. Use the push hoe to keep weeds down. *Do not* allow worn out crops to hold the land, running to seed and using fertilizer the next crop can use.

A vegetable garden which stands in water after rain needs draining. A wet soil is a cold soil so make certain the drainage is adequate.

By experimenting, discover which varieties suit the soil; buy the best seed available, it is the cheapest in the long run. Sow when the soil is warm and in a friable condition, do not be tempted into too early sowing by unseasonable spells of mild weather early in the year.

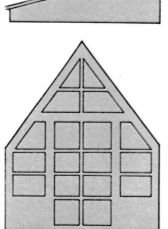

Select List

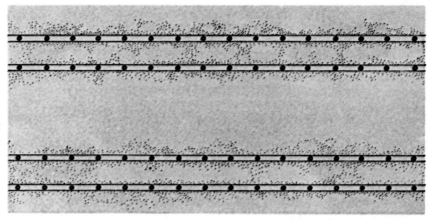

Broad Bean

Broad Beans are divided into two main classes: 'Windsors' which are the best flavoured but are tender and can not be sown early so are used for main and late crops; 'Longpods', though with not quite the flavour, can be sown very early, or even in Autumn to Winter.

Dwarf varieties make a third group, excellent for small gardens or catch cropping. As they follow a well manured crop apply a general fertilizer at only 2 oz per square yard (70 g/m²).

Sow early Spring onwards in double rows, 10 inches (25 cm) apart, 9 inches (23 cm) between the seeds with 30 inches (75 cm) between the double rows. A half-pint (0·3 litre) sows a double row 20 ft (6·1 m) long.

Aphis, remove the tops and spray with Derris.

Peas

Peas enjoy a rich soil with plenty of moisture in dry weather, and a supply of lime. Manure left over from the potatoes acts as a reservoir of moisture, and a dusting of lime between the rows supplies the other need. A dressing of superphosphate 3 days before sowing and a side dress-

wide 2–3 inches (5–8 cm) deep. Space the seeds in this 2 inches (5 cm) apart, 3 rows across the trench or drill. Cover with 1–2 inches (3–5 cm) of soil. Distance between rows varies. Dwarf earlies 18 inches (45 cm). 2nd earlies 2 ft (60 cm). Maincrop 3 ft (90 cm).

Support the haulms as they grow with twiggy sticks, canes, or nets; they crop better than if left unstaked.

Keep the rows weed free then, as the pods start to set, pinch out the tip of the growing point. This encourages the pods to fill and reduces the risk of infection by black fly. The tips if clean may be cooked and served with butter as a change from spinach.

When the crop is cleared cut the haulm for the compost heap leaving the nitrogen-rich roots to rot.

Varieties:
  'Aqua Dulce' for Autumn sowing.
  'Windsors' for flavour.
  'Rentpayer' for exhibition.
  'The Midget' for the small garden.
Diseases:
Chocolate Spot, spray with Bordeaux, but look to feeding and soil conditions.

ing of nitrogen for the early varieties when they are 2 or 3 inches (5–8 cm) high will be beneficial.

Sowing begins in early Spring and continues until mid Summer. ½ pint (0·3 litre) sows a row 30 ft (9·1 m) long. Sow in a flat bottomed trench, skimmed out with a spade 8 inches (20 cm)

Varieties:
  Earlies: 'Meteor', 'Little Marvel', 'Feltham First'. 1½ ft (45 cm) high.
  2nd Early: 'Early Onward', 'Green Shaft'. 2½ ft (75 cm) high.
  Maincrop: 'Alderman', 5 ft (1·5 m); 'Onward', 3 ft (90 cm) high.

Runner Beans

No crop responds so well to deep digging and manuring. Open up a trench in Autumn 2 ft (60 cm) deep; any spare manure or compost goes into it until late

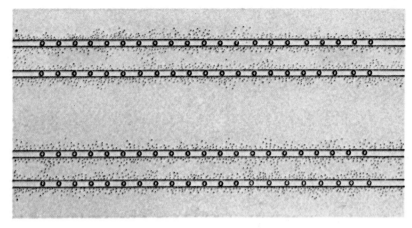

Winter when the soil is replaced. This long exposure to frost leaves the soil in a friable condition. Apply a dusting of lime if required. Sow seed under glass in peat pots during late Spring for planting out early Summer. Properly cared for this sowing will continue cropping until the first frost. Direct sowing may be made into double rows 15 inches (38 cm) apart, 12 inches (30 cm) between seeds. Double rows are spaced 5 ft (1·5 m) apart.

Pick the pods while young and tender, remove all the larger ones to stop the plant setting seed and going out of crop.

Water and liquid feed during dry weather. Support is given by strong poles and string (*see diagram*).

Garden Beetroot

Avoid land which has been freshly manured. When growing long beet soil must be deeply worked, but for globe varieties single spit cultivation will be enough. A little of the powdered seaweed fertilizer may be incorporated at the same time, or two weeks before sowing. Seed drills are drawn 12 inches (30 cm) apart, 1 inch (3 cm) deep. Sow at intervals from mid Spring to early Summer to give a succession of tender roots. For storage the roots are lifted before the first frost and packed between layers of sand in a clamp outdoors or a dry shed. Do not cut the tops before storing, twist them off not too close to the crown or bleeding will be excessive.

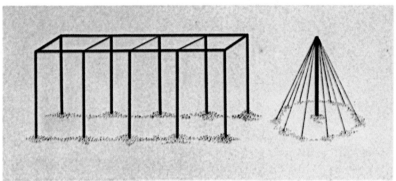

French Beans

A useful vegetable for limited space. Sow in drills under cloche or when the soil is warm in late Spring. Double rows 12 inches (30 cm) apart, 2 inches (5 cm) deep for early crops with the seeds spaced at 6 inches (15 cm) apart, thinned so the plants eventually stand 12 inches (30 cm) apart. Double rows spaced 2 ft (60 cm) apart.

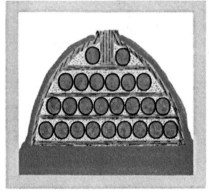

Beetroot varieties:
    Globe: 'Crimson Globe', 'Detroit', 'Little Ball'.
    Long rooted: 'Cheltenham Green Top'.

Brussels Sprouts

The old country adage that Brussels sprouts should be planted in land so firm the holes have to be made with a crow bar is not very far from the truth. Loose, freshly manured soil produces soft growth and 'blown' sprouts.

Prepare the soil in Autumn for Spring planting, rake in a base dressing of 1.1.1. fish meal two weeks before planting to pro-

mote sturdy balanced growth. Sow in mid Spring outdoors unless sprouts are required early, in which case sowing of 'Peer Gynt' may be made in a frame in late Winter.

Select the strongest seedlings, allowing 30 inches (75 cm) between plants and rows. Stronger varieties may need 36 inches (90 cm) to crop well. Earth up as growth proceeds (*see top right*). Start picking from the bottom of the stem.
Varieties:
    Early: 'Peer Gynt', 'Early Dwarf'.
    Maincrop: 'Cambridge No. 3', 'Exhibition'.
    Late: 'Market Rearguard', 'Citadel'.
Pests: The main problem is root fly. Felt discs around the stem at soil level or a B.H.C. root dip at planting time should give a control.

Cabbage (Spring)

Seed sown in mid Summer will provide plants for lining out in early Autumn. A dressing of lime may be necessary if potatoes occupied the land during the Summer, but no fertilizer which encourages soft growth must be used or winter losses will be heavy. A side dressing of nitrogen in Spring is all the spring cab-

bage requires. Space the plants 15 inches (38 cm) apart, 15 inches (38 cm) between rows.
Varieties:
    'Flower of Spring', 'Harbinger' (possibly the hardiest).

Cabbage (Summer)

Sow seed in late Winter under glass for early work, and direct into the open ground for maincrop. Planting distance varies, for 'Canon Ball' 12×12 inches (30 ×30 cm) is enough, while 'Winningstadt' requires 24×24 inches (60×60 cm). Other varieties: 'Stonehead' and 'Babyhead'.

Savoys and Winter Cabbage

Sow the seed in drills in late Spring and early Summer, transplant to soil which has not been freshly manured in mid Summer. No extra feeding should be necessary. Cultivations are weed control and pulling up extra soil around the stems the first few weeks after planting.

Varieties:
    'Christmas Drumhead', 'Dwarf Christmas Drumhead', 'January King'.
    'Winter White' has the advantage in that the heads can be pulled and stored in a cellar until required.
Pests: Cabbage Root Fly, control as for Brussels sprouts.

Cauliflower

Top quality heads are only produced on plants which are grown in soil which is highly fertile, well supplied with humus so it holds moisture during dry

weather. A dressing of fish meal fertilizer two weeks before planting would also encourage strong growth. Lime if required.

Seed should be sown at intervals beginning in late Winter under glass, continuing during mid and late Spring outdoors with winter varieties. At no stage must there be a check to the plants growth, a common cause of button curd.

Plants are spaced out at 24 inches (60 cm) each way, care being taken to protect the roots against root fly. Make sure there is no shortage of water during dry periods. As the curds develop a few outer leaves should be bent over to protect them from direct sunlight.
Varieties:
    Summer: 'All the Year Round', 'Early Snowball', 'Dominant'.
    Autumn: 'Dwarf Monarch', 'Vietchs Self Protecting'.
    Winter: 'Snows Winter White', 'Thanet', 'Manston', 'Continuity'.

Sprouting Broccoli

Sprouting Broccoli is one of the most delicious vegetables picked straight from the garden.

Seed sown in mid Spring will give plants for lining out a month later.

Allow 24–30 inches (60–75 cm) between individuals, 30 inches (75 cm) between the rows.

Varieties:

Autumn: 'Autumn Spear'.
Spring: 'Purple Sprouting'.
Spring: 'White Sprouting'.

Carrots

Carrots are really a light land crop, but will succeed on any soil which is well drained and deeply worked. Avoid using a soil which has been recently dressed with fresh manure — this could cause 'fanging' and 'bearded' roots. Rake a general fertilizer dressing into the soil 2 weeks before sowing — in the ratio of 1 nitrogen, 3 superphosphate, 2 potash. Sow in shallow drills $\frac{3}{4}$ inch (2 cm) deep, 12 inches (30 cm) apart.

On really heavy soils draw the drills deeper, and fill up to the required depth with sand. To avoid having to thin the seedlings, which often encourages carrot root fly, mix the seed with brick dust or dry sand and sow that for even distribution.

Maincrop carrots should be spaced about 4 inches (10 cm) apart. A dressing of soot down the rows improves root colour and acts as a carrot fly repellent. Paraffin mixed with sand is also a deterrent to the pest. Lift and store as for beetroot between layers of sand.
Varieties:

Earlies: 'Early Nantes', 'Amsterdam Forcing'.
Maincrop: 'Chantenay Red Core', 'Scarlet Perfection', 'New Red Intermediate'.

Celery

To grow really strong well flavoured sticks the crop should be grown in specially prepared trenches. Dig out trenches 20 inches (50 cm) deep by 20 inches (50 cm) wide. Fork in a dressing of strawy manure or compost into the bottom, then replace the excavated soil mixing in well rotted manure or compost at the same time. For those who can obtain a supply, rotten bracken is ideal.

Seed may be sown in mid Spring into seed trays of John Innes seed compost, and kept under glass in a temperature of 60°F (16°C).

Prick out into larger containers when the seedlings are large enough to handle.

Planting in prepared trenches takes place early to mid Summer at 10 inch (25 cm) intervals. Water in dry weather and spraying overhead in the evening is beneficial. Dusting the foliage with old soot reduces the risk of an attack from celery fly.

A general purpose fertilizer or liquid feed once the plants are growing is recommended. Remove side growths and weeds. Earthing up will give well

blanched sticks for the table, but collars are an alternative method. Work the soil in around the base of the plants — 4 inch (10 cm) layers at a time spreading the work over two months or even longer. After earthing up is completed the first sticks will be ready in 6 weeks.
Varieties:

'Prizetaker', 'Giant Pink'.
Self blanching: 'Golden Self Blanching', 'American Green'.
Diseases: Leaf Spot; seed is usually treated against it but if attack occurs spray with Bordeaux mixture.

Cucumber

Make up a bed in a frame or sheltered corner with well rotted manure or compost and good garden soil. The finished level should be 6 inches (15 cm) above that of the surrounding soil. This helps improve drainage, so preventing an attack of collar rot.

Sow the seed in early Spring for frame planting, or mid Spring for outdoor cultivation, singly in 3 inch (8 cm) pots. John Innes No. 1 compost would be suitable. When large enough, plant out under frames or cloches.

Syringe the plants over at least once every day. Liquid feed or top dress immediately a white

network of roots is seen throughout the bed.

Cut the fruits as they are large enough. In some varieties under frame cultivation some de-leafing may be necessary.
Varieties:
'Telegraph Improved', 'Pepinex' (all female flowers), 'Conqueror'.
Ridge Varieties: 'Burpee Hybrid'.

Lettuce

One of the essential crops for every kitchen garden. Sow in succession to provide crisp succulent heads throughout the season.

Soil must be well cultivated and rich in organic matter. It is best following a crop which has been well manured, for example potatoes. In the small garden it can usually be used as an intercrop, or even catch crop whenever space is available.

There are numerous varieties of lettuce on offer. All can be grouped under two main headings: *Cos* which is largely a Summer crop, and *Cabbage* lettuce which by careful selection of varieties can be enjoyed all the year round.

Only lettuces grown quickly in fertile soil provide crisp, sweet heads for table use. So make certain the soil is rich in humus and that once planted up is never allowed to dry out.

Summer lettuce: sow short rows at fortnightly intervals from mid Spring until early Autumn.

In Autumn make sowings under cloches to overwinter,

and in frames for use up to mid Winter.

Greenhouse cultivation will keep up the supply during the Winter months.
Suitable Varieties:
'Tom Thumb', excellent for early sowing.
'Buttercrunch', best for flavour.
'Sugar Cos', crisp fleshy hearts.
'May Queen', for greenhouse or frames.
'Webbs Wonderful', stands well without seeding.
'Winter Crop', hardy for outdoor sowings in Autumn.

Leeks

Because they are so hardy, leeks are an essential Winter vegetable. They are hardy enough to remain unharmed by the most severe weather.

The seeds are sown outdoors during early Spring except in very cold districts when it is safer to sow in a frame. Then when the plants are 4–6 inches (10–15 cm) high transplant them into rows 12 inches (30 cm) apart with the plants spaced 6 inches (15 cm) apart.

Land recently cleared of early potatoes or peas should crop well with leeks as it is fertile and moisture retentive.

Make the holes with a dibber some 4–6 inches (10–15 cm) deep; drop the plants into these and water well.

Keep the plants clear of weed. Earth up as with celery to increase the length of blanched stem.
Varieties:
'Prizetaker', 'Marble Pillar'.

Onions

An indispensable vegetable for flavourings in stews and sauces or as a main dish. A sunny and open though not windswept site is ideal.

Trench the bed in Autumn, working in a heavy dressing of rotted manure or compost. Onions may be grown on the same plot year after year so that fertility is built up.

Sow the seed immediately the soil is workable and warm outdoors, or in early Spring under glass. To ensure even distribution of the seed, mix it with dry sand or whitening powder.

Thin seedlings when large enough to handle, leaving them 9 inches (22 cm) apart. The spacing is the same if transplanting with 12 inches (30 cm) between the rows. Keep the rows weed-free. Feed at fortnightly intervals with a balanced liquid fertilizer until mid Summer.

Encourage the bulbs to ripen when full grown by bending the tops over and drawing the soil away from the bulbs to expose them to the sun.

Lift the bulbs and lay them out on a path to dry before storing in a cool well ventillated shed.

Spring Onions

To keep a supply of succulent salad onions throughout Summer and Autumn sow seeds in drills 12 inches (30 cm) apart, in soil prepared as for bulb onions. Three sowings at monthly intervals of rows 8 ft (2·4 m) long should see a family of four through to mid Autumn.
Variety:
    'White Lisbon'.

Marrow and Courgette

Sow the seed singly in peat pots under glass, or on a kitchen windowsill in mid Spring. Seedlings will be large enough to go outdoors in early Summer.

Make up raised mounds in a sheltered place in the garden by putting down a forkful of manure or compost then covering it with soil. Marrows enjoy a humus rich soil, plenty of moisture, and regular feeding. Grown on a compost heap or manure heap they will crop very heavily.

Cut the marrows while still small and cook them whole.

Radish

To produce well flavoured crisp roots, radish must grow quickly to maturity. Sow the seed $\frac{1}{2}$ inch (13 mm) deep in well cultivated soil, not too rich, choosing a site which is slightly shaded during the hottest part of the day.

Useful as an intercrop between slower growing vegetables, for example parsnips, celery and peas.

Sow at 14 day intervals from early Spring to early Autumn in 5 ft (1·5 m) rows.

Spinach

A good stand-by vegetable particularly for Summer use. Two types are available: *round-seeded* for the Summer, *prickly seeded* for the Winter.

Sow the Summer supply in a sheltered border in mid Spring. Keep well watered or it runs to seed. Winter spinach needs a well drained, well prepared, but not too rich, soil. By protecting part of the row with a cloche a continuous supply can be maintained throughout the Winter.

Sweet Corn

Sow the seed singly in peat pots in mid Spring to provide stock for planting out in late Spring — early Summer. Outdoor sowings may also be made under cloche in late Spring direct where they are to crop.

The soil should be well supplied with humus; the old rule 'hot at the top, moist at the root' applies very much if well filled cobs are to be cut.

Plant in blocks, *not long rows*, 15 inches (38 cm) between the plants by 24 inches (60 cm).

Block planting is essential to ensure pollination.

Keep the weeds down; mulch with peat or compost to keep the soil cool and moist.

Gather the cobs when the individual corns ooze a milky substance when squeezed but are already golden.
Varieties:
    'North Star', 'John Innes Hybrid'.

Parsnips

Parsnips need deeply cultivated soil which has not been manured for twelve months.

Sow the seed in shallow drills, 15 inches (38 cm) apart, from early to late Spring. Because the seed germinates slowly and weed control can be a problem, sow an indicator, e.g. radish, to mark the line of the rows. This makes push hoeing feasible.

Parsnips should be left in the ground until ready for use.

Tomatoes

No Summer crop is quite so universally appreciated, for salads, sandwiches, soups, or even stuffed as a main course.

In a heated greenhouse seed may be sown in John Innes No. 1, or one of the peat-based composts in late Winter, either direct into peat pots or first into tomato trays, then pricked off into small pots. The final planting can either be into tomato rings, deep boxes, or direct into the open border.

Soil should be changed each year to avoid a build up of pests and diseases, collectively referred to as soil sickness.

The modern method of growing plants in polythene bags or modules filled with a suitable compost has much to recommend it for this reason.

Do not force the plants too much at an early stage with over-feeding. The feeding commences as the first truss sets and fruit starts to swell.

The plants should be tapped when in flower, or shaken gently to sprinkle the pollen from sta-

mens to stigma ensuring a good set of fruit.

Damp overhead with a fine spray immediately afterwards.

Keep all unwanted side shoots pinched out. Tie the plants in to a cane or similar support.

For planting outdoors sow the seed under glass in mid Spring to provide sturdy seedlings for planting in a sheltered position outdoors in early Summer.

Ring culture. A layer of weathered boiler ash or gravel 4–6 inches (10–15 cm) thick is spread on the floor of the greenhouse. Standard, bottomless tomato rings are stood on this filled with John Innes No. 2 compost, or peat based compost.

The plants go into the rings and are then grown on. Water is applied to the ash or gravel to encourage root development while the liquid feed is given fortnightly direct to the ring.

Suitable varieties for flavour:

'Ailsa Craig', needs shade and extra potash or develops green back on the fruit.

'M.M.' or 'Moneymaker', reliable heavy cropper.

'Golden Queen', delicious sweet flavour.

'The Amateur', for outdoors.

'Tiny Tim', for window boxes.

Potatoes

One of the best crops for breaking in virgin soil or cleaning dirty land.

Prepare the soil with heavy dressings of manure or compost in Autumn, leave the surface rough to weather.

Before planting, the tubers may be set up in trays, then placed in a light moderately

warm place to sprout or 'chit'.

Early varieties may be planted in a sheltered bed outdoors during early Spring spaced 18 inches (45 cm) between tubers, 18 to 24 inches (45–60 cm) between the rows. Maincrop varieties go in during mid and late Spring at 20 to 24 inches (50–60 cm) apart. Plant 4 inches (10 cm) deep then, as growth proceeds, draw up the soil (earth up) on either side to protect the tubers as they form from the light.

In districts where blight is a problem spray with Bordeaux mixture or similar compound in mid to late Summer. Choose a variety to suit the soil.

Varieties:

'Arran Pilot' and 'Home Guard' are reliable earlies.

'Majestic' is the most reliable main crop.

Herbs

Herbs are both useful and ornamental. Choose a well drained, sheltered border close to the house and near the kitchen, otherwise they will not be used. A position in full sun, but with some shade during the hottest part of the day, is ideal.

Soil should be light and well drained. Seed may be sown either under glass or, in the case of parsley, direct where they are to grow.

Annual herbs mature quickly so need very good growing conditions. Mint, tarragon, or horse radish are obtained as roots, not grown from seed, and prefer to be in light shade.

Herbs for drying are gathered at the peak of perfection just as the flower buds show in the morning, after the dew has lifted but before the sun is really hot. Make up the bunches and place in an airy shed to dry. Failing this an empty room in the house, or a brief period in a cool oven will do.

Balm; used for cooking with chicken or certain fish — grayling.

Basil; for mixing with cheese spreads, tomatoes or sauces.

Sweet Basil; just a few chopped leaves in salads.

Chervil; imparts a delicate flavour to egg dishes.

Dill; for fish dishes, cucumber and pickles.

Marjoram "Pot"; with meat or fish and vegetable soups.

Marjoram Sweet; adds continental flavour to meat, fish and salads.

Parsley; sow in an open position and use as required in sauces, soups or salads.

Sage; ornamental shrubs used with all greasy meat dishes.

Savory, Summer & Winter; Combines well with all bean dishes.

Thyme; a beautiful carpeting shrub suitable for bouquet garni or rich shell fish dishes.

Herbs add an old world quality to the garden apart from their beauty of flower or foliage. Their fragrance is reminiscent of a more leisurely age when gardens themselves possessed that timeless quality of changing changelessness. For this alone they would be worthy of a place in the garden.

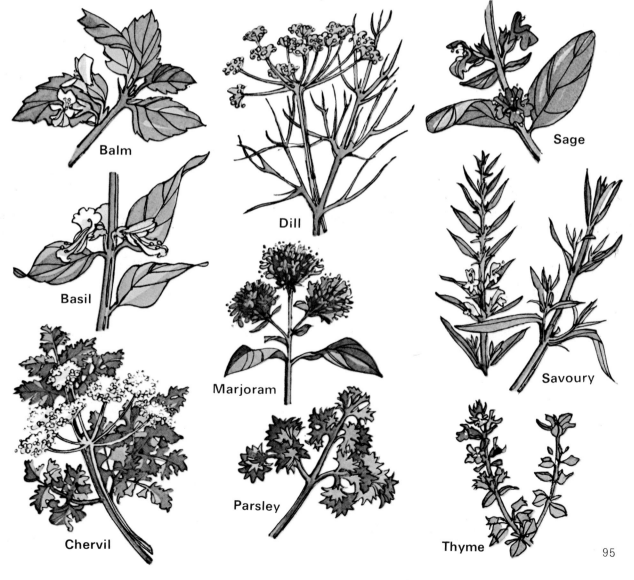

Balm

Dill

Sage

Basil

Marjoram

Savoury

Chervil

Parsley

Thyme

Fruit

Fruit growing is not just the preserve of the specialist professional. Increasing numbers of amateurs are finding it an interesting and a rewarding hobby. Fruit picked and eaten full ripe from the garden is an experience to anticipate.

In modern gardens the area which can be devoted entirely to fruit growing is limited to such an extent that whatever the soil it can be sufficiently improved to crop well. By double digging, combined with heavy dressings of organic matter, any but the most poorly drained soil from heavy clays to light sand will grow quality fruit.

Choose the most sheltered bed the garden offers provided it is not in an area where frost gathers. Cold air flows down hill, if a wall or hedge impedes air movement the frost builds up like water behind a dam. I have seen trees half way up a slope with blossom intact after a cold night while those at the bottom were black ruin.

Make sure the soil is free from perennial weeds, important during the establishing years for top fruit, even more with soft fruit which have to be clean cultivated. If the soil is 'dirty' double dig and manure, then take a cleaning crop of potatoes or brassica and plant fruit the following Autumn.

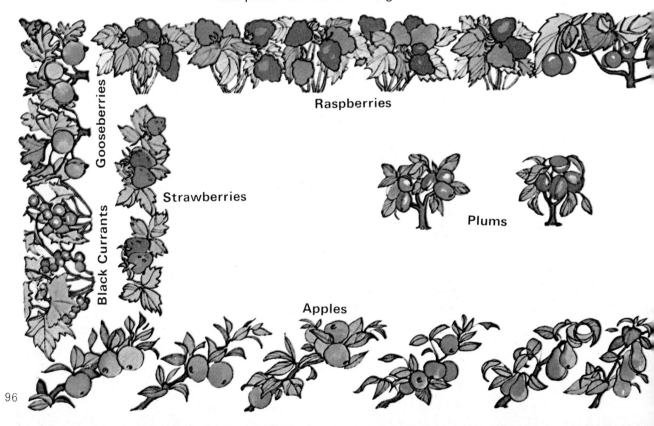

Gooseberries

Raspberries

Strawberries

Black Currants

Plums

Apples

Points to Remember

Make sure the drainage is good — wet soils are sour and cold.

Make sure the soil is well worked and manured.

Make sure there is shelter, but not frost pooling.

Exposure to cold winds checks growth and prevents the pollinating insects doing their work so fruit does not set.

Make sure that, if apple, pears, plums or cherries are to be grown, there is no hard 'pan' of soil to a depth of 3 feet (90 cm) which will impede root penetration. A pick makes short work of this when planting holes are being prepared.

Most fruits prefer a soil just the acid side of neutral, so a reading may be made to check the pH. Lime sweetens acid soils, improves the physical texture, and neutralises the organic acids. An excess brings a risk of chlorosis due to mineral deficiencies.

Add lime to acid soils. Use dressings of organic manure and sulphate of ammonia to reduce the lime content of alkaline soils. Fertility of the orchard can be maintained by regular fertilizer dressing adjusted to the type of fruit being grown, plus mulches of compost.

Within Broad Limits:

Dessert apples, gooseberries, raspberries need high potash to give the fruit good colour and flavour.

Cooking apples, pears, plums, blackcurrants and Morello cherries need a higher ratio of nitrogen compared to potash.

All need a balanced feed in the formative years after planting with superphosphate to assist the formation of a good root system. An analysis of Nit 7, Superphosphate 8, Potash 6, would suit newly planted top fruit well for the first 3 years. Apply 2 oz (60 g) in early Spring and again in early Summer after fruit has set.

When to Plant

During the dormant season whenever the soil condition and weather permits. Avoid late Spring planting or growth may have already started. For *strawberries*, the only evergreen, I prefer early Autumn planting providing certified stock is obtainable. Soil is still warm enough for the runners to take hold before Winter.

As with ornamental shrubs, take out a hole large enough to accommodate the roots comfortably after first cutting away any which are damaged or broken. Adjust the depth of the root so the soil mark is about 1 inch (2–3 cm) below the surface (Soil mark shows the level of planting in the nursery). *Staking,* especially with trees on dwarfing stocks (stock described later), will almost certainly be necessary. Use a standard stake, treated with a wood preservative, placed in position before planting or use a cane as marker to avoid root damage (see Trees and Shrubs, page 41). Tie with a patent tree tie, two for a half standard; three ties may be required to keep a standard secure. Firm well but leave the surface soil loose so rain penetrates readily.

Apple Rootstocks

The vigour of the stock on which the apple varieties is worked will govern (1) eventual size and vigour of tree, (2) how long it takes to come into crop bearing.

East Malling Experimental Station has contributed a great deal of valuable information on fruit growing, not least in research done to discover the most suitable root stocks to use in a given situation.

M9 In a good soil is an all round quality stock which gives a small easily managed tree that comes into bearing in three years.

M106 is slightly more vigorous and would be advisable in soils not up to the standard M9 demands. Possibly may take an extra year to start cropping.

Malling III is a very vigorous stock normally used for standards where tree size is immaterial and heavy cropping is the prime requisite.

Trained forms e.g. dwarf pyramids, cordons, espaliers are usually worked on *M9*.

Pear Rootstocks

Quince C is the stock which is used in some cases for trained forms on good soils. Quince A is slightly more vigorous and comes into crop almost as quickly so is more reliable over a wide range of soils.

Specify the rootstock required, it is important. Do not accept trees on unnamed seedling stocks of doubtful vigour. Trees may be bought at almost any age up to fruiting. The enthusiast will prefer to buy a maiden, one year old, to train. Young trees suffer less shock on transplanting and cost less, but take more work and longer to come into crop.

Two-year-old trees have been cut back to make side branches break to form a head.

Sweet Cherries

Morello Cherries

Red Currants

ears

Hard Fruit

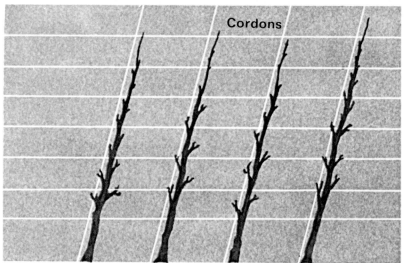

Cordons

Dwarf Pyramid

Various Forms of Tree

Cordon, single: A fruit tree restricted to one stem (double cordon has two). Apples grown by this method are usually worked on *M9* or pears on Quince C or A.

The usual method is to train the stem obliquely onto wires stretched taut between supports *(see above)*.

All growths except the terminal leader are pruned back in late Summer to 5 leaves, in late Autumn these are pruned again to 3–4 buds *(see bottom right)*. Rows are best run north to south so each side of the row gets a share of sunlight. Space the trees in rows 30 inches (90 cm) apart. Excellent as a screen between vegetables and flower garden.

Dwarf pyramids on *M9* single upright stem with short branches radiating out in all directions. Something halfway between an espalier and cordon. Plant 8 ft (2·4 m) apart *(see left)*.

Espalier. Posts with wires strained between them 18 inches (45 cm) apart *(upper right)*. Single stemmed apples or pears are planted at 12 ft (3·7 m) spacing on wires, and side branches are pulled down and grown along the wires to fill the intervening space.

Dwarf bush as the name implies has a clear stem of 18 to 24 inches (45–60 cm) before branching. Space these in the garden at 12 ft (3·7 m) apart.

Fan trained trees may be grown on wires but frequently a wall is used as the support *(centre right)*. 5 branches per side, 10 overall is considered a well furnished fan.

Pollination

Not all varieties will give a full crop of fruit unless cross pollinated by another compatible variety flowering at the same time. When in doubt consult the nursery who supply the trees, they will make suggestions. In fact, cropping of all varieties will be improved if adequate provision is made for cross pollination. The following are suitable:

Culinary

'Grenadier' Flowers mid season, ripens early Autumn — one of the best for small garden.

'Arthur Turner' Flowers early mid season, needs only enough pruning to keep the tree centre open. Ripens Autumn.

'James Grieve' Flowers mid season, a good pollinater, but flesh is too acid for dessert purposes.

'Rev. Wilkes' Flowers early, season late Autumn, a good small garden variety.

'Lane's Prince Albert' Flowers late, fruit will keep until early Spring.

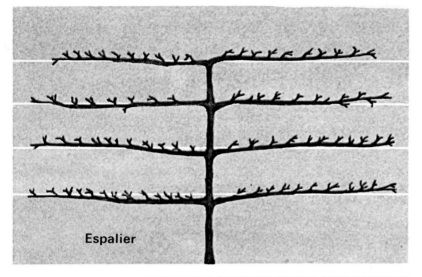

Espalier

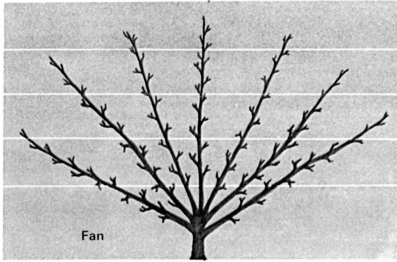

Fan

'Bramley's Seedling' Flowers mid season, will keep until Spring. No use as a pollinator, and because it is such a strong grower must be on a dwarf stock in a small garden.

Dessert

'Worcester Pearmain' Though a tip fruiting variety is still worth a place. Flowers late, ripe in early Autumn.

'Epicure' Flowers mid season, ripens in early Autumn. Needs to be eaten straight from the tree.

'Lord Lambourne' Flowers in mid season, good reliable variety. Late Autumn.

'Charles Ross' Flowers mid season, fruit very large unless feeding is adjusted. Late Autumn—Winter.

'Ribston Pippin' Flowers early and sometimes gets caught by frost. Neat growth which makes it suitable for the small garden. Late Autumn—Winter.

'Sunset' Flowers mid season, a useful keeping variety for colder climates. Winter.

'Cox's Orange Pippin' Flowers mid season, early into crop as a young tree. Winter.

'Winston' Flowers mid season, does best as an espalier or cordon. Late Winter—Spring.

The spray programme against pests or diseases depends on locality, soil and variety, so must be adjusted accordingly. A tar oil will clean up the trees, applied during mid—late Winter, controls aphis and suckers.

Derris—pyrethrum during the growing season is a safe insecticide for Codling moth, aphis, sawfly. Failing this, *B.H.C.*

Karathane and *Captan* or *Zineb* formulations are suitable for mildew and scab.

Winter Pruning

In the early years Winter pruning concentrates on producing a well shaped bush. After the framework is established pruning linked with feeding aims at encouraging fruit bud formation, making spraying easier, and in general maintaining the tree in full productive good health.

Spur pruning: Branch leader is pruned to continue growth, laterals from main stem are cut back to make them form fruit buds.

Tip bearers, for example, 'Worcester Pearmain' form fruit buds on unpruned laterals, so build up a central framework which is allowed to develop unpruned laterals and natural spurs.

Pears are best grown as cordons, espaliers, or dwarf pyramids on Quince A or C rootstock. They like a fairly heavy soil and will not thrive on light land unless well supplied with moisture.

Varieties: Some, because they will not form a union directly with quince, have to be double worked. For example, 'Jargonelle' is not compatible with a quince stock, so is first grafted onto a bridge of 'Beurre Hardy' which will unite with stock and scion. (*See illustration*).

Selected varieties:
'Jargonelle' Mid season flowering — ripe late Summer.
'Beurre Hardy' Late flowering season Autumn.
'Conference' Mid season flowering, self fertile almost. Season late Autumn. A first choice for most gardens, though not the best texture and flavour.
'William Bon Chretien' Blossoms mid season, ripens for eating in Autumn. Bottles and cans well.
'Doyenne du Comice' Flowers late so needs 'Beurre Hardy' to cross pollinate. Ripens irregularly from early Autumn, so check at intervals. The pear for outstanding flavour.
'Monarch' Flowers mid season. Useful as a cordon. Will keep

until mid Winter. *Cross pollination is essential with most pears, so two or more varieties must be grown.*

On trained forms, cordons etc, once the frame is made, prune in late Summer all side shoots back to 4 leaves.
Winter wash as for apples. Derris pyrethrum or B.H.C. in Summer. Two sprays with Captan should control pear scab.

Plums like a deep moisture retentive soil, rich in nitrogen with lime added to help stoning. As the plum flowers very early a frost-free sheltered position is to be advised.

As with apples and pears a root stock is necessary to give some measure of control over growth. Root stocks for plums are limited. Possibly 'St Julien' (A) is best for all-round worth, with 'Mussel' as a second choice, though it is prone to suckering.

Some varieties are self fertile, others are sterile to their own

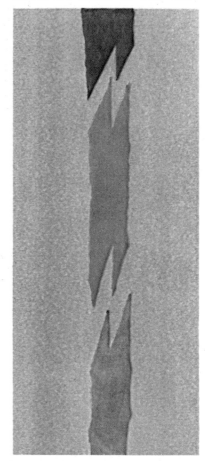

pollen, so again care must be taken in variety selection. Plums are usually grown as half standards because of the rather weeping habit of the branches which would sweep the ground otherwise. Do not prune unless absolutely necessary in which case work may be done when the crop is picked, then all wounds sealed against silver leaf fungus with Stockholm Tar.
Varieties:
'Victoria' Dual purpose, late Summer—early Autumn. Flowers mid season and is very fertile.
'Denniston's Superb Gage' Dessert. Self fertile, mid season blossom, fruit ripe late Summer.
'Early Transparent Gage' Dessert. Self fertile, early flowering, ripens late Summer.
'Czar' Cooker. Mid season flowering, ripens late Summer.
'Warwickshire Drooper' Cooker. Flowers mid season. Growth neat and for a plum, compact. Ready early Autumn.
Use a winter wash as for apples in the dormant season. Derris pyrethrum sprays in summer.

Cherries are divided into two groups — the sweet dessert varieties and the acid 'Morello' which are splendid for making jam and bottling and which can be grown on a north wall. They are only worth growing on a wall or fence as fan trained trees where they can be netted against birds.
The sweet cherry is almost self sterile, but all can be cross pollinated by the 'Morello' group. Cherries are budded onto *Malling F12/1* rootstock. Wall fans are spaced 12 ft (3·7 m) apart.
Varieties:
'Gov Wood', 'Merton Glory', 'Early Rivers', 'Morello' for cross pollination.

Spray with tar oil in Winter against aphis.

Soft Fruit

Blackcurrants are a very worthwhile garden crop, the weight of fruit in return for garden space occupied is considerable.

Almost any soil will grow blackcurrants providing it has been well dug and manured. Mulching in Summer to retain moisture, combined with nitrogen feeding, will do much to ensure a heavy crop. Blackcurrants flower early so a sheltered, frost-free site is required to protect the flowers and allow pollinating insects to work. Unlike pears or apples, blackcurrants root readily from cuttings or layers. Hardwood cuttings are taken from bushes which have been noted during the Summer as free from virus diseases, also the insect pest which causes big bud. Cuttings of one-year-old shoots, 10 inches (25 cm) long or thereabouts are lined out in sandy soil in early Autumn (*below*). Leave all the buds on, for as many shoots as possible are required to grow from below soil level. 7 inches (18 cm) of the length goes below soil level.

Planting with either rooted cuttings or bought-in certified stock takes place in Autumn. Use only the best material available. Firm them in well, leaving no bare area of stem exposed above soil level. Space the bushes 5 ft (1·5 m) apart in the rows. Cut all the shoots hard back to soil level, one bud only being left from which strong growth breaks the following year.

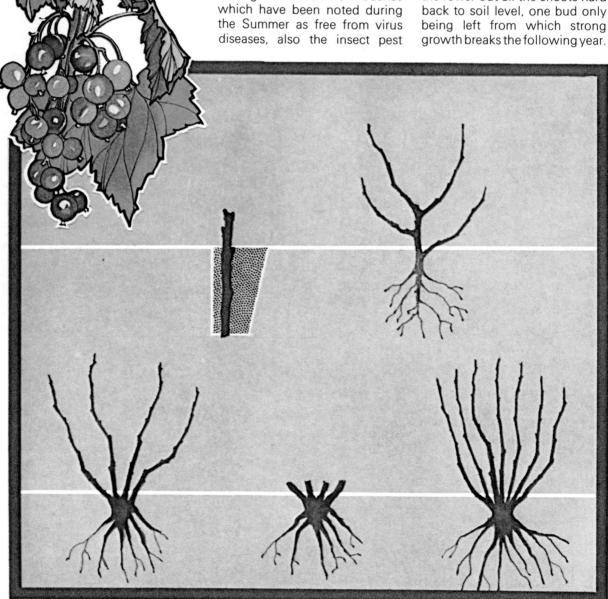

Once established, approximately a third of the bush is pruned away each year taking branches right out at the base to make way for strong fruiting wood.

Varieties:
'Wellington XXX', 'Mendip Cross', 'Baldwin'.

Pests: big bud mite, remove and burn enlarged bud.

Diseases: Mildew, spray with Benomyl or Dithane.

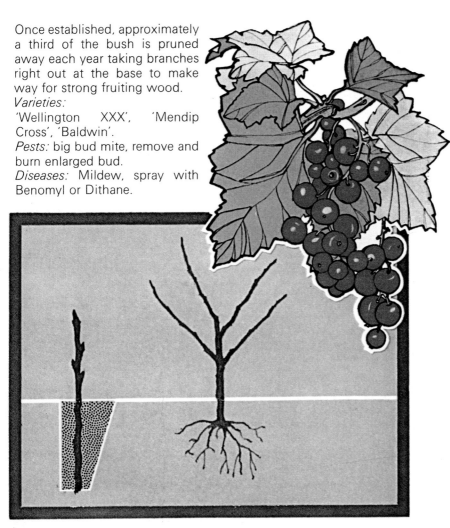

north wall, usually a part of the garden that is difficult to make productive. The fruit however does not have the flavour that it develops in warmer conditions. Both red and white currants are propagated by hard wood cuttings about 10 inches (25 cm) long. The cuttings are taken with the heel in mid Autumn. Remove all the buds except the top four. Strong shoots will then break from these but a clean stem of 6 inches (15 cm) is left above soil level. This helps to keep the berries up and prevents them being soiled by splashes from the soil under heavy rain. Where space only permits the growth of one or two bushes then these should be restricted to varieties of red colour 'Laxtons No. 1', 'Earliest of Four lands' and 'Red Lake'. The white currants are rather more difficult to keep in crop every year. Usually it is considered a pretty good average to get a crop every other year. Varieties include 'White Grape', which is a mid season fruiting variety, and 'White Leviathan', a slightly later cropping variety.

Red and White Currants

Both red and white currants will grow well as cordons and, where space is at a premium, this makes a very satisfactory method particularly for the small garden as usually only a few pounds of fruit are required. Because they fruit on spurs growing from the old wood, this shoot formation is encouraged when the plants are grown as cordons up to 5 feet (1·5 m) high, then each year the side shoots are cut back to two buds. A mulch of compost or well rotted farm yard manure helps to keep the bushes growing strongly and, although the demand for nitrogen is not as high as it is in black currants, this extra additional feeding does encourage shoot formation. A careful watch should be kept out for any signs of potash deficiency because red and white currants are particularly susceptible to a shortage of this vital element. Red currants and white currants have the additional advantage of cropping well on a

Raspberries prefer a soil which is freely drained and well supplied with humus, so they develop fully the fibrous roots system necessary for healthy cane production. Light soils need heavy dressings of manure to hold moisture.

Choose a sheltered site free from late frosts and strong winds. Buy *virus free certified stock.* Make sure the land is free of perennial weeds before planting as raspberries are so shallow rooting, that excessive weed control after planting will do damage. Weeds can be controlled with Paraquat, also unwanted suckers. Plant early Autumn 18 inches (45 cm) apart, supporting the canes on horizontal wires strung between strong posts.

After planting cut all the canes back to 6 inches (15 cm) above soil level. Strong shoots will break in Spring, these should be thinned to the required number (5) spaced evenly out along the supporting wire. In Spring the canes which are to fruit may be topped, this encourages the fruiting laterals. Cut out the old stem which remains, once suckers have broken. Each year the old canes which have fruited are cut out and new ones tied in to replace them.

Nitrogen is given at the rate of 1 oz per square yard (35g/m^2), potash 2 oz (70g/m^2) each Spring, followed by a mulch of compost in early Summer.
Varieties:
'Malling Promise', 'Glen Clova', 'Lloyd George', 'Norfolk Giant'.

Gooseberries prefer a medium or moderately heavy, weed-free, deeply worked soil. Choose a fairly sheltered site, for the flowers open early. Light overhead shade will help, or grow the bushes as double cordons on a fence.
Propagation: By hardwood cuttings taken in early Autumn made from one-year-old shoots about 8–10 inches (20–25 cm) long. Rub out the lower buds so, as with red currants, the bushes are on a short clean stem. (See illustration.) Before planting make sure all suckers below the branches are removed.
Planting distance: Bushes 4–5 ft (1·2–1·5 m). Cordons 15 inches (38 cm). Double cordons 3 ft (90 cm).
Feeding with a complete high nitrogen fertilizer in Spring bal-

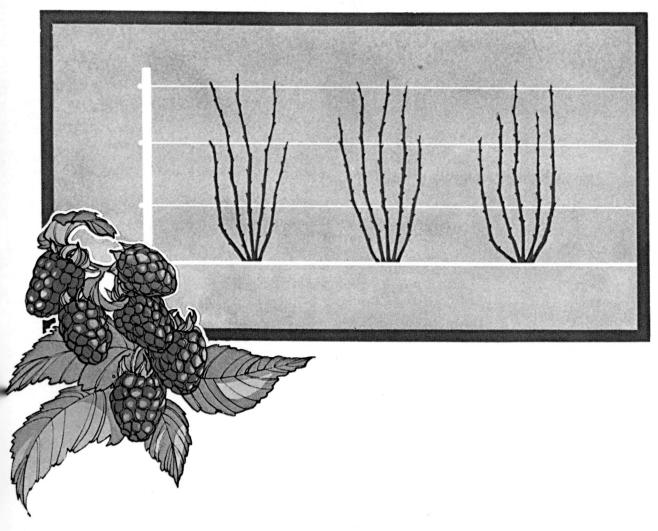

anced by extra potash in early Summer if growth is too soft. This lush growth encourages mildew. Mulch with compost in late Spring.

Pests: Sawfly, spray in mid Spring with Derris-Pyrethrum, repeat 3–4 weeks later, or hand pick the caterpillars.

Diseases: American gooseberry mildew, spray with Benomyl at flower bud stage, repeat two or three times at 2-week intervals.

Varieties:
'Careless', early, white
'Leveller', early, yellow
'Lancer', late, green
'Lancashire Lad', mid season, red
'Whinhams Industry', mid season, red

Strawberries like a rich soil well supplied with humus and not liable to dry out during the Summer. Prepare the soil by double digging working in all the manure and compost available. Make certain *no* Perennial weeds are left.

Secrets of Success
Heavy composting. Adequate watering in dry weather. Removing excess runners and weeds. Slightly acid soil. Keep in a bed with good frost drainage but sheltered from wind. Buy *virus free stock*, plant in early Autumn while the soil is still warm. Space 18 inches (45 cm) by 24 inches (60 cm) apart. The junction between leaves and roots should be exactly at soil level. Plant firm or frost during Winter can lift the plants out. Feeding with fish meal at 2 oz per square yard (70 g/m²) in early Spring. Remove flower trusses the first year so plants become well settled in. Remove runners unless these are required to start a new bed elsewhere. Straw, peat, or similar material is placed down the rows to keep the fruit from becoming soiled.

Varieties:
'Royal Sovereign', unsurpassed for flavour, 'Grandee', and 'Cambridge Favourite'.

Diseases: Botrytis — spray with Benomyl according to makers' instructions.

Indoor Plants for House and Greenhouse

The cultivation of plants in pots can enable people who live in flats to follow the hobby of gardening in a practical way. In addition to providing an interest they are extremely decorative.

Though many plants will put up with considerable variations in temperature, extremes should be avoided. For example, living room conditions which rise to 75–80°F (24–27°C) during the evening and fall to near freezing by early morning will test the resilience of even the most durable pot plant.

A low average temperature which shows little fluctuation between night and day time is more tolerable to the plant than one which alternates between tropical and freezing.

Cyclamen and poinsettia are two of the most popular of all pot plants for culturing indoors in the home. They display their colour at the time of the year when colour is in short supply.

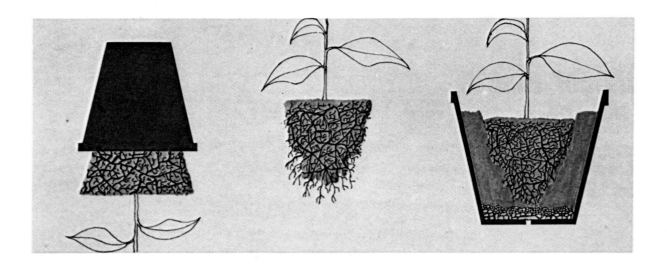

Humidity

Dry air is bad for most green-house and house plants, causing leaf discoloration, de-hydration, and ultimately death. Air in a cool room is usually relatively more humid than the air in a centrally heated room maintained at 70°F (21°C).

Plants grown in the hot dry conditions of the average living room should be provided with a tray of moist pebbles or peat to stand on. The moisture from the peat or pebbles creates a local micro-climate of humid air around the plant. Alternatively, choose plants which will tolerate the dry conditions.

The ideal, of course, is to have a trough in which the pots can be plunged up to their rims in moist peat during their time indoors. When the plant shows signs of discomfort it can be given a rest in a cooler room or greenhouse.

Light

In a greenhouse, provided the glass is kept clean, this presents no problems. Indoors, most plants prefer good indirect light, but so long as shade is given during the hottest part of the day in Summer, direct sunlight rarely harms them. *Intense shade causes spindly growth.*

Ventilation

Good air circulation as described in the chapter on greenhouses is important, and this also applies with house plants. Supply fresh air whenever weather conditions permit, but *avoid draughts, no plant will tolerate them.*

Watering

How frequent watering is necessary depends on:

a. The type of plant: a *Primula obconica* needs moister soil than a *Billbergia nutans*.

b. The season: pots which need watering twice a week in Summer may only require moisture once a month in Winter.

c. The growing conditions: high temperature and in consequence dry air increase a plant's moisture demand.

d. The compost and container: The peat-based compost in a plastic pot needs careful watering or it becomes too wet. The ideal is to maintain the soil in an evenly moist state. Too dry and the plants wilt, too wet results in a cold airless soil in which roots die.

Never water in driblets from above, stand the whole pot in a sink or similar container full of water so the root ball is soaked. In a correctly made compost the surplus drains away.

Repotting

Repotting (*see above*) is required when the roots become pot bound. With quick growing plants this may happen the first year, others may carry on two years or more with just a top dressing.

Knock the root out of the pot. Tease out the lower roots and re-pot in a slightly larger *clean* pot which has some pebbles or broken pot at the bottom for drainage, and use the same type of compost the plant was originally potted into. Immediately after potting, water thoroughly by soaking.

Feeding

Feeding will be necessary with most plants about 6–8 weeks after repotting. Then twice a month will be sufficient using a balanced feed according to the makers' instructions. *Do not over feed* or the plant will go sick.

Cleaning

Syringe the plants over every day or two with tepid water to help keep the foliage fresh and free from dust. Stand the pots in the bath so that the work can be done thoroughly. There are proprietory substances on the market which, used according to the manufacturers' instructions, will keep the foliage bright and healthy looking.

Indoor Plants

Plants should never be subject to unnecessary exposure between the place of purchase and the home, especially in Winter. Get the vendor to wrap them well, take them home immediately and there will be no check to growth. In the nursery plants are grown under carefully controlled conditions, so sudden exposure to the vagaries of a Winter's day can be fatal.

Many house plants root readily from cuttings. A seed box with a clear polythene or perspex lid makes a splendid propagator, especially if bottom heat can be supplied. The methods used are described under the individual plants.

There are some beautiful containers available which enable the plants to be grouped together, making the provision of a suitably humid climate and watering easier. A bold group makes a more effective room decoration than individual plants scattered about the house in a haphazard way.

Trellis work can be fitted to walls to support climbing plants. Fit trays underneath the pots to

prevent drips damaging the furniture or carpets. Wall brackets, jardinières, wooden tubs and troughs are in themselves ornamental, filled with plants they make a room into a garden.

Artificial light can be used to assist plants to be grown in positions which would otherwise be too dark. Carefully sited fluorescent tubes will help plants to flower but must be kept on for ten to twelve hours a day if they are the sole source of light. Glass cases fitted with lights can be just as much a feature as an aquarium.

Plants grouped together inside a glass or plastic container, the bottle garden or terrarium

Hanging baskets add interest in character to a sun porch or loggia but regular attention must be paid to watering and feeding otherwise the compost is soon exhausted (*left*).

technique, is a solution to plant growing where the air is very dry in a centrally heated building.

A glass carboy thoroughly cleaned, an aquarium, goldfish bowl, bon-bon jar, in fact any container with glass sides will do. The neck should be large enough for the small cuttings to be passed inside.

Begin by placing a layer of charcoal on the base of the container. Add either John Innes or one of the peat-based composts. Leave the level uneven so it can be landscaped with small stones or pieces of cork bark.

Choose plants which will not quickly outgrow the container such as Cryptanthus, Peperomia, Asplenium, Fittonia, Calathea, Maranta, Hedera (Ivy), Ficus pumila, Dracaena.

Once planted up, water, then seal the container and stand away from direct sunlight. Fluorescent tube illumination shows the bottle garden or terrarium to good advantage.

Select List

Aphelandra squarrosa 'Louisae' "Zebra Plant" has considerable value as a foliage plant, in addition to the plume of long lasting yellow flowers. The veins of the leaves are strongly outlined in white. Remarkably tolerant of average living room conditions but, like most plants, it infinitely prefers the higher humidity of the greenhouse. Stem cuttings inserted in sandy compost over bottom heat root easily.

Aechmea fasciata "Urn Plant" is one of those strikingly attractive plants which it is worth making an effort to grow really well. The most suitable room in the house which they can share with the *Saintpaulia* "African Violet" is the bathroom. Though they will tolerate living room conditions they often refuse to flower, which reduces their value.

Leaves are greyish green stripped and flecked with silver. The spikey flower head is a mixture of blue, red and silver which persists for several months. Water freely, and spray overhead in Summer, but do not over-water in Winter.

Propagation is by means of offsets which are removed with a sharp knife, and rooted in sphagnum moss and sand, or by means of seed. These are then potted up in the growing mixture of equal parts loam, peat and coarse sand. Failing this John Innes or one of the peat-based mixtures suits very well.

Left
Italian vases and similar ornamental containers can be planted up to add seasonal interest to terraces and gravel drives in front of the house.

Beloperone guttata "Shrimp Plant". In all its colour forms is possessed of a curiously compelling attraction. The shrimp-like flower bracts persist for several months in both the pink and cream forms.

John Innes or peat-based compost, and plenty of moisture during the Summer, are all that is required to grow this plant successfully. Half ripe cuttings root readily.

Begonia semperflorens is frequently grown as a Summer bedding plant. They do succeed well as pot plants in either a greenhouse or a well lit room where their long flowering period may be appreciated. Plants in the home are sometimes difficult to bring through the Winter. Ordinary compost, John Innes, or peat-based.

Propagation by seed or cuttings is easy enough to make this a commendably useful plant.

Billbergia nutans, the most commonly grown of the Bromeliads, has pendulous tubular flowers curiously shaded pink, yellow, blue and green. The leaves are long and tough, characteristic of the whole family.

A compost of 1 loam, 1 peat, 1 sand, or one of the peat-based mixtures, suits this adaptable plant very well. Crock the pots well to ensure free drainage.

Cyclamen need humid, draught-free conditions and a moderate temperature which remains fairly constant between 55 and 65°F (13–18°C). Water by plunging the pots up to the rim as required.

Standard, John Innes and peat-based composts suit very well. After flowering, allow the foliage to yellow and the corm to ripen, for storing until late Summer when it may be watered to promote growth once more.

Fuchsia hybrids "Lady's Pendant" will grow reasonably well in cool, well ventilated rooms, but are better suited with greenhouse conditions. If the atmosphere is too dry the flowers fall without opening and the foliage turns yellow.

John Innes or the peat-based compost are acceptable.

Water copiously during the flowering season and feed as the plants come into flower at 10 day intervals.

Cuttings of young side shoots will root quickly inserted in sandy compost.

Euphorbia "Poinsettia" is one of the most rewarding of flowering pot plants, for with care the brilliantly coloured leafy bracts are there for several months. A light airy position and adequate moisture are all that is required to succeed with this excellent plant. Cut it back hard as the leaves yellow.

Cuttings may be made from the young growths which, taken into sandy compost then enclosed in a polythene bag, will root a reasonable percentage.

Gloxinia, now known as *Sinningia*, produce velvet textured flowers in late Summer and early Autumn. The colour varies from scarlet through purple to white.

Tubers may be started into growth during late Winter – early Spring, planted hollow side up in peat-based compost. Alternatively, seed may be sown in mid Winter to provide plants for flowering in early Autumn. Prick off as the second leaf shows, then pot on as required.

After flowering, do not water to dry the tubers off for storing during the Winter.

Campanula isophylla "Italian Bellflower" given even modest attention will flower throughout the Summer, both blue and white forms have this admirable virtue. A cool equable temperature is to be preferred, away from direct sunlight. Water freely during the growing season but reduce the supply in Winter. Cuttings in early Summer root readily.

Hoya carnosa "Wax Flower" is an attractive climber which, in warm moist conditions, has a profusion of thick petalled wax-like creamy white flowers.

Cuttings of side shoots or layers will give rooted plants.

Water well during the growing season but reduce the supply in Winter. In my experience the variegated leaved form is not so free flowering. All forms are best cultivated in a greenhouse.

Hydrangea hortensia need a cool airy position with copious watering during the growing season. Dry air and draughts are fatal.

A compost of 2 parts loam, 1 part peat, 1 sand, with a dusting of complete fertilizer is quite suitable.

To blue the flowers add a teaspoonful of alum to a gallon of soft water at each watering, or mix aluminium sulphate with the potting soil which should be free of lime.

Cuttings of young wood 3 to 6 inches (8–15 cm) long will strike from late Spring through Summer.

Impatiens hybrids "Busy Lizzie": few plants can have enjoyed such a meteoric rise in popularity. Possibly their extreme good nature is the explanation. They grow readily from seed, and cuttings placed in water will root with ridiculous ease.

The dwarf varieties 'Tom Thumb' and 'Elfin' are suitable for pot culture. A position away from direct sun and plenty of water during the flower season is all the plant requires.

Pelargonium "Geranium". The traditional plants of sunlit cottage windows where they can be persuaded to continue flowering for months on end. The Zonal and Ivy leaved can be had in many varieties. *P. peltatum* with red tinged variegated leaves and pink flowers, or the scented leaved *P. crispum* "Variegatum" are worthy of note.

A John Innes No. 2 compost, liquid feed, plenty of water and full light are the best recipe for success. During the resting period cool, dry, frost-free conditions.

Cuttings root easily throughout Spring and Summer.

Primula obconica. Those with a sensitive skin should be cautious, for the sap of some primulas can cause a painful rash.

Seed should be sown in early Spring for Winter flowering or in mid Summer to flower the following Spring. Grow the seedlings on in a cool shady frame during Summer.

Flowering is continuous for many weeks if the plants are given cool, light, airy conditions with adequate water.

Rhododendron "Azalea". Not the easiest of house plants, but an extremely popular florist's flower. Warm, humid, draught-free conditions are essential. A dry atmosphere causes both flowers and foliage to drop.

A compost of 2 parts peat, 1 part loam, and 1 part sand or any of the ready made mixtures which are lime-free can be used. Keep in cool, frost-free conditions until the buds show, then move the pots indoors for flowering.

Cuttings of half-matured shoots will root easily taken in summer.

Saintpaulia "African Violets" are better grown in a greenhouse, plantarium or aquarium. Failing these the bathroom offers the constant humidity and even temperature necessary to keep african violets happy.

A peaty compost is necessary to provide a cool moist root run. Propagation is by means of seed, or leaf cuttings.

Schlumbergera × *buckleyi* "Christmas Cactus" makes a popular pot plant, easily raised from cuttings broken at a joint and inserted around the rim of a pot filled with standard compost.

Excellent when grown in a hanging basket where the scarlet or pink flowers are displayed to full advantage from late Autumn well into Winter.

Adequate water during the flowering season, plus liquid feeding will keep this plant in good health. Do not dry off, even in the resting period keep the soil moist.

Foliage Plants

Begonia are a large genus, notable for species with both handsome leaves and attractive flowers. *Begonia rex* is outstanding, the leaves are patterned in a wide range of colours: silver, red, pink, purple and green. They need a constant temperature and humidity, being absolutely intolerant of dry air.

Shade from direct sunlight and water copiously during the growing period. Propagation is by leaf cuttings. One of the standard made-up compost mixtures suits very well.

Calathea and *Maranta* are extremely decorative foliage plants which, given reasonable attention, are useful pot plants.

They are suitable for bottle garden planting, particularly where the beautifully patterned leaves develop their full potential. They prefer warm humid conditions; hot dry air or draughts destroy the leaves very quickly.

Water freely in Spring and Summer, keep them cooler and drier in Winter. A standard compost with charcoal added suits very well. Propagation by division or leaf cuttings.

Chlorophytum elatum 'Variegatum'. Compost — John Innes No. 1 or peat mixture. Grow in full light and buoyant conditions so the long narrow green and white banded leaves develop their full beauty.

Adequate water should be given from early Spring to late Autumn, slightly less in Winter, but never allow the soil to become completely dry.

Propagation is by pegging down the young plantlets which appear on the ends of long stems into small pots filled with compost.

Cissus antartica "Kangaroo Vine" makes a most tolerant house plant, and is equally ornamental in the greenhouse. The dark shiny green leaves are serrated at the margins.

John Innes or peat-based composts are suitable potting mixtures. Keep well watered during the Summer, just comfortably moist in Winter. Shade from direct sunshine in mid Summer.

John Innes No. 2 potting mixture suits the plant's needs. Grow in light airy conditions and a constant temperature. Avoid dry, hot air or direct sunlight in Summer. Water freely in Summer, rather less in Winter but do not dry off altogether. Propagation by off-shoots as they appear.

Coleus. Because they grow so readily and in such rich coloured variety from seed they enjoy a certain popularity. Their cultivation under average household conditions is not easy and they are best accommodated in a greenhouse.

The nettle-like leaves are mottled sometimes with three or four colour shades — yellow, red, green and purple. Flowers should be nipped as they develop or they spoil the shape of the parent plant.

John Innes or the peat composts are suitable. Adequate moisture and freedom from frost are two basic essentials.

Seed sown in mid Winter, or tip cuttings of side shoots rooted in late Summer, form a ready means of propagation.

Dracaena sanderiana. The slightly undulate leaves, glaucous grey with creamy white margins are most attractive.

× *Fatshedera lizei* 'Variegata' is a result of a cross between Ivy and a Fatsia as the name implies. Though eventually the plant grows very large it is popular as a house plant because of the way it adapts to room conditions.

Grow in John Innes or peat compost. They do not mind some shade, but require plenty of water, humid air and freedom from frost. Propagate by means of side shoots in mid to late Summer.

Ficus elastica 'Decora' "India Rubber Plant". The dark glossy green leaves make a most impressive room decoration. Copious waterings are needed during the Summer, rather less in Winter. Keep the atmosphere humid or a plant with such a large leaf is rapidly dehydrated. Sponge the leaves to free them from dust at regular intervals, and weak liquid feed every 10 days.

Propagation by cuttings of lateral shoots taken during late Spring/early Summer will root if inserted in a pot filled with sandy compost enclosed in a polythene bag.

Hedera "Ivy" make excellent cool room house plants, particularly the forms of *H. helix* which are quite hardy outdoors.

Cuttings of most ivies will root easily. Insert tips of shoots 3–4 inches (8–10 cm) long in sand during Summer months, then place in a sealed polythene bag or closed frame. Pot off when rooted into John Innes compost, then when the roots fill the pots apply a weak liquid feed at 10 day intervals during the growing season mid Spring — early Autumn.

Ivy will do well in partial shade and should be kept away from direct sunlight.

Hedera canariensis 'Variegata' is a vigorous climber suitable for growing on a patio trellis. *Hedera helix* 'Glacier' has small leaves marbled with grey and edged with white. *H. helix* 'Green Ripple' and 'Buttercup' are two of the most useful varieties for pot culture.

Maranta leuconeura 'Kerchoveana' popularly known as prayer plant because its leaves stand upright and together at night. The foliage is apple green with purple markings.
M. leuconeura 'Massangeana' "Fishbone Plant" has white veined leaves. They will grow well in either John Innes or peat-based compost and need repotting at regular intervals.

Propagation is by division in mid-late Spring. Cuttings of basal shoots taken in late Summer offer an alternative method. A humid climate is essential which is why Maranta grow well in bottle gardens. Under living room conditions syringe over daily.
Peperomia make pleasing but rather tender house plants, the rat-tail flowers appear during late Summer.

Grow them in John Innes or peat-based compost, but as the root system is small, under, rather than over pot them. Avoid dry air and draughts and do not over-water, especially in Winter when the compost may be allowed to dry out on the surface.

A humid atmosphere in Summer is essential when cuttings taken between late Spring and late Summer will root readily in a mixture of 2 sand, 1 peat.

Peperomia argyreia has thick fleshy leaves, silver grey with dark green bands. *Peperomia scandens* is a trailing plant with pale green cream-margin heart-shaped leaves.

Philodendron scandens. A climber with heart-shaped leaves which will put up with a marked degree of atmospheric pollution.

Peat-based composts suit them, and the pots should stand on moist pebbles or peat to give a suitably humid micro-climate, and water freely from mid Spring to mid Autumn, but only moderately during Winter. Keep the plants in a light airy position but away from direct sunlight.

Cuttings of growing points taken in early Summer are one method of increasing one's stock of plants.

John Innes compost with a liquid feed at 14 day intervals during the Summer, and annual repotting will keep the plant in good health.

Cuttings of side shoots taken in late Spring are one method of propagation.

Pilea cadierei 'Nana' "Friendship" or "Aluminium" plant makes a neat pot plant, the dark green leaves are attractively marked with silver. Shade from bright sunlight, give plenty of water in Summer but keep the soil only just moist in Winter.

A dilute liquid feed at ten day intervals during the Summer will be beneficial. Stem cuttings 3–4 inches (8–10 cm) long will root if inserted in a sandy compost.

Tradescantia fluminensis 'Quicksilver' is easily cultivated, the leaves are beautifully striped with silver. Keep them in a light airy place away from direct sunlight.

John Innes compost is a suitable growing medium, but they will need regular watering and feeding during the period mid Spring to early Autumn. Keep slightly moist over Winter.

Cuttings root easily taken at any time during the growing period.

Rhoicissus rhomboidea is popular for its foliage and enjoys a fairly shady position free from atmospheric pollution.

Zebrina pendula is best grown in a hanging basket in a window facing west.

The proprietory peat-based composts are suitable, supplemented by liquid feeds every 14 days during Summer. Keep soil just moist in Winter. Tip cuttings taken during early and mid Summer will root readily in sandy compost.

Pests and Diseases

As with human ailments, the best control for both pests and diseases in plants is to prevent, so far as is possible, allowing conditions to develop which encourage infestation. Healthy, contentedly growing plants, properly cared for in a well tilled soil, will present few problems. Work on the principle that fungicides and insecticides are expensive to buy and apply. So cure the cause not the complaint. Indeed, some of the chemicals used in the garden, if carelessly applied, do more harm than the pest or disease itself.

There are times when even in the best maintained garden a slug or greenfly dares to intrude, or mildew to desecrate the smooth, polished expanse of a healthy leaf.

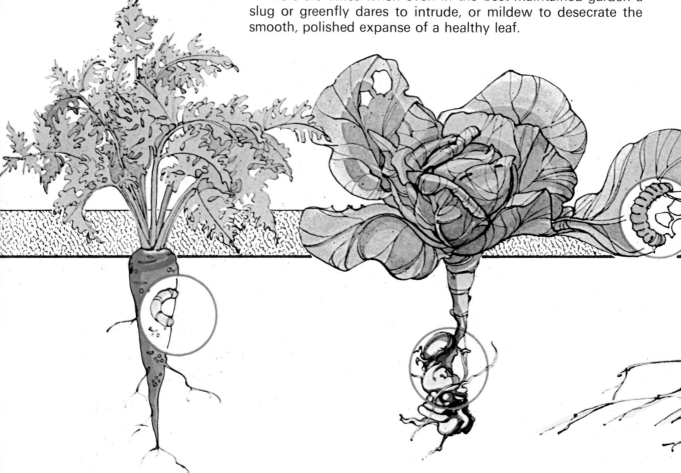

Carrot root fly bores holes in carrots turning them rusty brown; foliage wilts and withers.

Cabbages can be attacked by *club root* disease and caterpillars.

Tomato plants are vulnerable to *slugs, white-fly* and *blossom end rot.*

Red spider mite, black aphis and *tulip fire* can cause serious damage to plants like the tulip.

Corrective Treatment

Control is easier with some understanding of the feeding habits of the pest, for instance a different spray may be needed for an insect with a biting mouth-piece (weevils), than for one which pierces a leaf and sucks the sap (greenfly).

For a 'biter', a dust or spray applied to the leaf surface ensures that a lethal dose of poison is taken in during routine feeding. Possibly a better guide would be to say dust or spray applied to the area in which the pest feeds; root, stem, leaf or flower.

Examples would be: dipping the roots in a paste made up of proprietory compounds based on B.H.C. would help to control cabbage-root fly. Knowledge that the fly needs to lay eggs

close to the stem means that infestation can be avoided by growing the plant through a three inch (8 cm) square tarred felt disk. The caterpillars are prevented from reaching the roots by the disk, and chemical control is then unnecessary.

'Borers' such as slugs, codling moth, wireworms, and woodlice, with a little ingenuity and knowledge of their habits, can be trapped or poisoned with judiciously placed poison baits at feeding points near resting places or nests.

Insecticides are of two types. Contact, where the pest must actually come into contact with the spray or dust, for example, greenfly controls. Stomach poisons, which are sprayed on the food supply and taken in when feeding; these are weevil controls.

A modern refinement, the systemic insecticide, where the chemical is absorbed so it circulates in the plant's sap stream, will control any susceptible pest which feeds on the treated plant.

Fungicides control fungus diseases as the name implies. Most of the treatments aim at prevention rather than cure, so once again some knowledge of the life history of the disease helps to achieve the best results. For instance tomato mildew usually appears in mid Summer so, to prevent an attack, start to spray in early Summer, continuing at 14 day intervals until the crop is cleared.

Dollar spot, a disease on grass, can be controlled if treated immediately the symptoms (round brown patches on the lawn) appear. One of the several dressings available or a systemic fungicide will do the trick.

Combined seed dressings which contain both a fungicide and insecticide give protection to young germinating seedlings during the vulnerable juvenile stage. These dressings are being used increasingly by seed firms before the seed is packeted.

Poison baits, principally used against slugs, snails, woodlice, earwigs, rats and mice, can be harmful to wildlife or domestic pets so should not be used indiscriminately. Put the bait in positions readily accessible to

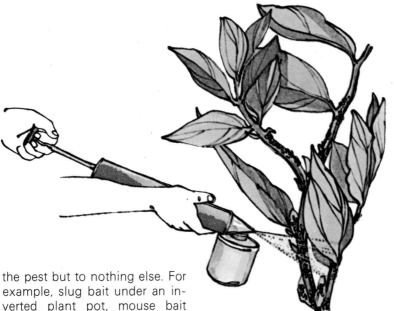

the pest but to nothing else. For example, slug bait under an inverted plant pot, mouse bait inside a section of drainage tile.

Sometimes pests can be deterred by a noxious (to them at least) smell. Moth balls or tar oil poked into mole runs will banish the nuisance. Cats and dogs are repelled by impregnated pellets placed at vantage points around the garden.

Virus diseases are impossible to identify except by the damage they cause. Once infection has taken place the gardener must destroy the host plant to prevent the disease spreading through the whole crop. Do not propagate from virus infected plants. Control insect vectors which carry the disease to healthy plants. Guard against infection by buying stock only from a reputable source. Burn obviously infected plants immediately to stop the disease spreading.

Deficiency diseases have symptoms very similar to those caused by virus, to the amateur eye, but are due to an absence of some essential mineral, not to disease. Usually the quantity of each element required is minute, and may be corrected by direct application. For example, one teaspoonful of Epsom Salts in a gallon of water will correct Magnesium deficiency symptoms on half-a-dozen roses. Iron deficiency is common in some plants growing on lime soils; the element can be purchased in a soluble form and applied as a solution.

A soil well maintained with farm manure, compost, or similar organic matter rarely suffers from a mineral deficiency.

Golden Rules

1. Positively identify the pest or disease.
2. Buy the best material available to specifically correct the condition. Do not blanket spray with several chemicals on the off-chance one will do the trick.
3. Read the instructions twice so no mistake is possible with measuring the quantities. Do not add an extra measure just to make sure. *Obey* the manufacturers instructions absolutely.
4. Choose a windless dry day to apply the treatment.
5. Do not spray wide open flowers, or visiting bees and other useful insects may be killed.
6. Wash hands and spray equipment after use thoroughly.
7. Keep all chemicals in a locked cupboard away from children.

Disease resistance is important. For example, in certain soils it is advisable to grow 'Wilt Resistant Asters' or 'Rust Resistant Antirrhinums' in the Summer bedding scheme.

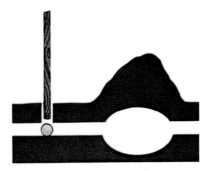

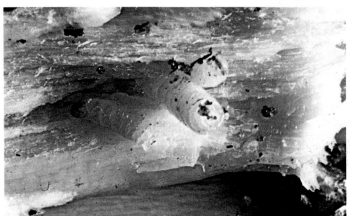

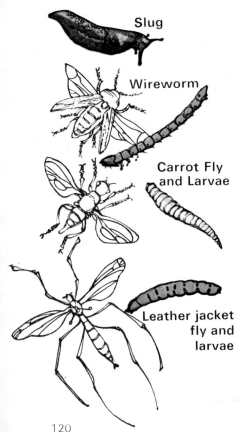

Slug

Wireworm

Carrot Fly
and Larvae

Leather jacket
fly and
larvae

Direct Attack

The black and white illustrations show the harmless parent-stage of the pests which cause the actual damage.

Slugs feed on plant tissue doing considerable damage. Hand pick them in late evening when they come out to feed. Heaps of proprietory pellets placed at strategic intervals under a piece of slate will account for a good number. Each morning the victims should be removed and burned or they may recover.

Wireworms: Larva of 'Click' beetle. Yellow brown, up to $\frac{3}{4}$ inch (2 cm) long, feed on underground parts of the plant i.e. root crops. Hand pick during digging, or control with wireworm dust, available from most sundriesmen.

Carrot Fly bores holes in the carrots turning them rusty brown; foliage wilts and withers. Grow onions between rows of carrots.

This kills the smell of carrots which attracts the fly. Paraffin impregnated sand serves the same purpose. Carrot seed can now be treated with a combined seed dressing.

Leather Jackets: Larvae of Crane Fly, brownish grey legless, feeds on grass roots. In lawns treat with 'Sevin' dust mixed with the autumn top dressing.

Soil-borne diseases can be cured by chemical sterilization in greenhouses by treating them with Formaldehyde or proprietory fumigants.

Damping-off disease in seedlings can be treated with Orthocide Captan, or in some cases by watering with systemic fungicide.

Cabbage Root Fly lays eggs near the stem of the plant. The resulting caterpillar causes damage to the leaf. Control by dipping roots in a B.H.C. — based compound.

Airborne Pests

Greenfly and Blackfly seriously weaken plants, distorting fruits and foliage by feeding on them. Against aphides, probably the most common pest, spray with

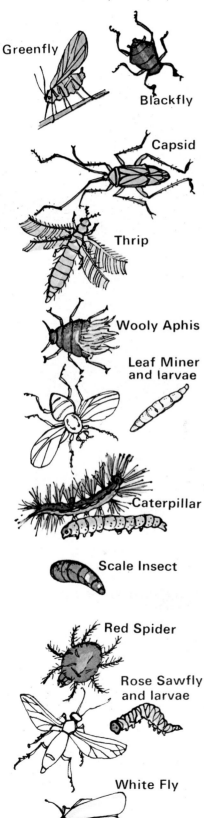

Greenfly

Blackfly

Capsid

Thrip

Wooly Aphis

Leaf Miner and larvae

Caterpillar

Scale Insect

Red Spider

Rose Sawfly and larvae

White Fly

Derris-pyrethrum combined with soft soap on food crops, and with one of the proprietory materials e.g. Sybol specifically made for the job on ornamentals. A systemic insecticide would possibly give good results in this respect. On fruit trees a winter wash kills overwintering eggs. Blackfly infestation on broad beans can be reduced by removing the growing point of the plants once the bottom flowers have set. The first eggs laid by the overwintering female aphis are always laid in the soft tip shoots of the bean.

Capsid causes brown spots and malformation of leaves and fruit by its feeding habits. On fruit trees apply a tar oil wash in the dormant season. On ornamental plants nicotine, Lindex, Derris/ soft soap, or systemic insecticide during the growing season.

Thrip cause spotting and silvering of leaves and flowers which, with a heavy infestation of the pest, may turn brown and distorted. The insects are minute so the first signs of attack are the pin hole marks in the leaves. Control with a systemic or Malathion. Under glass, aerosol or smoke generators of insecticide give the best results.

Woolly Aphis. Masses of White cotton wool like wax on the stems of trees indicate the pests' presence. They cause swollen and deformed growths. Paint with methylated spirits or spray with Mortegg winter wash. In Summer systemic insecticide or liquid Malathion will clear up an attack.

Soil-Borne Pests and Diseases

Crop rotation is the best insurance against fungus diseases and certain pests, especially in the vegetable plot. For example, to avoid potato eel worm never grow potatoes on the same land at less than four year intervals.

Keep the garden free of rubbish, heaps of rotting vegetable material, debris from previous crops left as ground keepers, old cabbages and sprout stools. *Burn diseased materials.*

Leaf Miner damage on celery and chrysanthemums, where the maggots tunnel inside the leaves is difficult to control. Spray the young plants with Lindane, Derris or liquid Malathion immediately the tunnels appear. A preventative spray in early/mid Spring and then three weeks later could prevent an attack occurring.

Caterpillars of many butterflies, sawfly and moths can cause serious damage by eating the leaves of host plants. Hand picking or a combined Derris pyrethrum plus soft soap spray will clear up the nuisance.

Scale Insects cause a loss of vigour by feeding on various parts of the host plant. The dried up body of the female filled with eggs make it look like a miniature tortoise. The best control is to paint with concentrated winter wash or methylated spirits. In Summer a systemic insecticide will exterminate them.

Red Spider are microscopic red mites only visible under a hand lens, but causing severe weakening of the host plant by sucking sap from the leaves, and in some cases causing defoliation. Spray with Derris, liquid Malathion or systemic insecticide, repeated ten days later.

Rose Sawfly caterpillars feed on the leaves skeletonising them, rendering the bushes unsightly. Apply Lindex, Derris, Sybol or systemic insecticide immediately the damage is seen.

White Fly are serious pests in some seasons of crops like tomatoes. Once established they breed so quickly any control must be repeated at regular intervals to ensure all survivors are killed before they breed. Greenhouse aerosols or smoke pellets ensure the chemical is carried to every crevice of the greenhouse. Malathion, nicotine and Derris sprays, providing the foliage is fully wetted on both sides, are alternative controls.

Cultural Disorders

Cultural disorders can largely be eliminated by good gardening. *Blossom End Rot* affects tomato plants growing in a rich soil and deprived of water just as the young fruit are forming. A hard leathery patch at the base of the fruit develops (*right*). On some soils the condition is aggravated by a shortage of lime. Control; do not feed until the bottom truss of fruit is swelling. Keep the plants well supplied with water. Check the pH to discover if the soil needs lime.

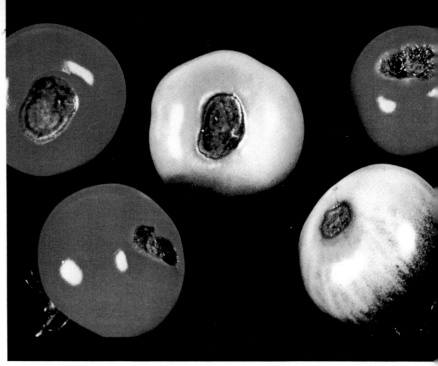

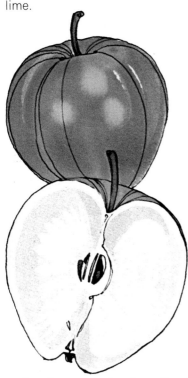

Another example of a cultural disorder, *Water Core* in apples occurs more frequently in soils fed with nitrogen than where a complete fertilizer dressing is used (*above*).

Gummosis is another cultural disorder occurring on stone fruits, cucumbers, and melons and is connected with nutrition and variations in temperature, both of which can be controlled by the gardener (*right*).

Fungus Diseases

Spray programmes must be planned to coincide with the most vulnerable stage in the disease's life cycle. Usually the chemical is applied so as to kill existing spores and leave a protective covering on the leaf which prevents any further infection. There is a promise that the new systemic fungicide absorbed into the sap stream of the plant will provide almost complete protection against specific diseases.

Bordeaux mixture is a useful general purpose fungicide controlling mildew, rust, potato blight, grey mould, leaf spot on celery and many other obnoxious diseases.

Captan, one of the newer fungicides is useful in controlling fruit diseases (apple mildew), corm rots, grey mould, damping off in chrysanthemums and bedding plants.

Formalin is used for soil sterilization in the cultivation of greenhouse crops particularly. The soil is watered with the chemical and then covered with sacks or polythene sheeting for four days. Soil so treated must not be used for three weeks.

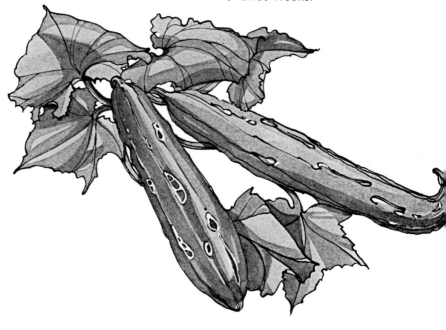

Lime Sulphur is used on fruit trees against scab, peach leaf curl, big bud mite, raspberry cane spot; and on ornamental plants: paeonia blight, chrysanthemum rust etc. As an alternative spray to lime sulphur on apples which are sulphur-shy, use *Captan. Left,* apple scab.

Sulphur is still a safe useful fungicide used to protect dahlia and begonia tubers in store over Winter against soft rot, rhizome rot on irises, neck rot of pot plants, and *Botrytis* on tulips. The modern control for *Botrytis* "Tulip Fire" (*below*) is now *Thiram*.

Rose diseases have a special significance as no plant is more universally grown in gardens. Rust, black spot and mildew (*left*) can be reduced by good cultivation, growing resistant varieties, and a regular spray programme. Proprietary mixtures based on *Thiram* are available; indeed, developments in the field of fungicides is so rapid that new chemicals appear annually. Apart from these, copper fungicide will keep rust in check, and sulphur based sprays at regular intervals will limit infection by mildew and black spot.

Weed Killers

A llowed to grow unchecked, weeds make the garden look untidy and harbour pests or diseases. In addition they compete with the crops for water, food, light and space. Annual weeds, possibly some perennials, for example nettle tops, make useful additions to the compost heap. Weeds dug into vegetable gardens or annual borders, provided they will not re-establish, act as green manure, Hoeing and mechanical methods should all.be employed to eliminate weeds as they appear. Choose a time when weather conditions are suitable. Sun and drying wind kill severed weeds before they can re-root.

Paraquat based weed killers which act only through the green colouring matter of the leaf are a new garden aid. The

The effectiveness of selective weed killers is well-demonstrated by the control experiment (above) *in which a section of grass was left untreated.*

chemically active agent is broken down on contact with the soil, planting of the border can take place without any delay. Paraquat based weed killers may be used as a chemical hoe amongst established shrubs, orchards, hedge bottoms, in fact, anywhere the weeds can be treated without splashing the foliage of the cultivated plants. As the paraquat acts only through the leaves it can be watered right up the woody stems of trees or shrubs.

Sodium chlorate, Simazine and similar total weed killers are useful where the land to be cleared of weeds is not needed for planting until at least six months have passed. Paths, drives and waste ground which are not, of course, intended for cropping may be treated in Spring. Care should be taken on sloping ground for the material may be washed out into the surrounding garden for, unlike paraquat, it is not broken down on contact with the soil.

Selective weed killers are especially useful on lawns as a control for undesirable broad leaved weeds. The broad leaved weeds are killed because they hold a lethal dose of the poison while the narrower leaved grass is unharmed. Use selective weed killers only on a still day, remember even the fumes can kill sensitive plants like tomatoes, and always thoroughly wash the container after use. Better still keep separate equipment for applying weed killers.

Lawn sand is not a selective weed killer in the strict sense of the word. It is made up of 20 parts by weight of lime-free sand, 3 parts sulphate of ammonia and 1 part calcined sulphate of iron. In addition to killing weeds it also helps keep moss in check. Apply the mixture at the rate of 3 ounces per square yard ($100 g/m^2$).

Avoid using any chemicals in the garden which will injure you, your pets, or wild life other than the pest to be eliminated.

Acknowledgements

Cover picture by S. J. Brown
of Norwich.

**I.C.I. Garden Products
Division** kindly supplied the
transparencies which appear
on pages 13, 25, 120, 122,
123, 124 and 125.

Bill Davidson's photographs
appear on pages 22, 30, 31,
33, 35, 36, 40, 42, 49, 56, 59,
64, 66, 70, 75, 81, 84, 85 and
106.

Syndication International:
photograph on page 101.